Navigating Today's Treacherous Markets

Central Bank Intervention, Rampant Insider Trading, "Bad" High Frequency Trading

By Chandra Kumar

Published by Gabbro Books

ISBN 978-967-12609-2-0

Table of Contents

Chapter 1 1

Treacherous Markets 1

Introduction 1

Individual Investor Participation 2

Governments and Central Banks 4

Insider Trading 8

Insider Trading Big Fish 10

Chapter 2 15

The Machines Are Here, Part 1:
Introducing Algorithmic Trading,
High Frequency Trading 15

What Is Algorithmic Trading? 15

What Is High Frequency Trading (HFT)? 17

Very High Speed (or Low Latency) 18

Very Short-Term, with No Positions Held Overnight.... 19

Individual Trades Involve Profits, Losses
and Volumes That Are Very Small..............................19

Trading Frequency Is Extremely High 20

Typically Involves Colocation.....................................20

The Great HFT Debate...**22**

Is HFT Making Markets More Treacherous?...........**22**

Chapter 3...*25*

The Machines Are Here, Part 2:
Into the Guts of HFT...*25*

HFT Strategies..**25**

Market Making... 25

Relative Value Arbitrage.. 27

Trend and Event-Based Strategies............................... 28

Spoofing, Layering, Momentum Ignition..................... 29

Latency Arbitrage, Quote Stuffing 30

The Nature and Effects of HFT..................................**31**

Manipulative HFT...**31**

Disruptive HFT...**33**

The Flash Crash 33

What Happened 34

Black Monday, October 1987: The Original
Flash Crash? 35

The Flash Crash Debate 37

Flash Crash and Black Monday: Differences and
Similarities 39

Mini Flash Crashes... 40

Other Disruptions/Glitches 42

Privileged HFT **43**

Special Order Types.. 44

Events-Based Trading.. 46

Special Data Feeds.. 48

Good HFT **48**

HFT Arbitrage... 49

HFT Market Making 49

Criticism of HFT Market Making 50

The HFT Scalper Model: A Discussion **54**

Chapter 4 .... *59*

The Machines Are Here, Part 3:
HFT and the Individual Investor *59*

Neutralizing Bad HFT **59**

Neutralizing Manipulative HFT 59

Neutralizing Disruptive HFT 60

Measures to Control Disruptive HFT 61

Why Are the LULD Rules and Circuit Breakers
Likely to Work? 63

HFT in Decline **64**

Winners and Losers in the Age of HFT **65**

Institutional Investors 66

Individual Short-Term Traders 67

Retail Investors Are Winners in the Age of HFT 68

**Leveling the Playing Field—What a
Novel Concept!** **69**

HFT and Individual Investor Confidence **70**

**Things About Machine Trading That
Bother the Average Investor** **71**

How Can HFTs Make Money Every Day? 71

With the Machines Taking Over, the
Average Investor Has No Chance! 72

HFT Is like Bacteria **73**

In Summary: Treacherous but Navigable **73**

Chapter 5 .... *75*

Individual Investors Navigating Today's Markets *75*

Introduction..75

Longer-Term Investing Is Where
You Should Be...77

Shorting Is Not for the Majority 80

Patiently Wait for the Bull............................82

Chapter 6 .... *85*

Rules of the Master Traders *85*

Introducing Trading Rules 85

Trading Rules to Live By 87

    1. Chill but Never Freeze........................... 87

    2. Poker Principles 88

    3. Always Have a Plan 91

    4. Don't Fight the Primary Trend............. 92

    5. Losers Average Losers 94

    6. You Should Feel Good *After* Entering
       a Position.. 94

7. Focus on the Target and
Stop Checking Prices 95

8. Prices Are Where They Are for a Reason 96

9. You Must Feel Uncomfortable 96

10. When You Find Yourself Asking for Advice,
You Know You're in Trouble 96

11. Don't Be Part of the Herd Except 97

12. If You're Not 100 Percent OK,
Take a Trading Break 97

13. Never Let Your Expectations
Make You Break Your Rules 98

14. Mental Rehearsal Is Important 99

15. Widely Anticipated Bad News,
When It Comes out, Will Send Markets Up 100

16. The Snake That's Going to Bite You
Is Not the One You're Watching 101

17. Boring, Sideways Markets
Will Empty Your Pockets 101

18. If You Have to Win, You Will Lose 102

19. Never Make a Mistake... 103

20. Never Let a Profit Become a Loss 103

21. Be a Lone Wolf 103

22. Have a Positive Mental Attitude 104

23. Get Position Size Right 105

24. Diversification Produces Average Results 106

25. Use If-Not-Correct (INC) Stops 107

26. Be Prepared to Leave Money on the Table........... 109

27. Learn to Cope with Losing Streaks 109

28. Enter as Others Capitulate 110

29. Keep Good Records... 110

30. Use Chart Patterns 111

Breaking the Rules **113**

1. If You Can Trade One Market,
You Can Trade Any Market................................ 114

2. It's Where You Sell That Counts........................... 116

3. It Never Hurts to Take Profits 116

Rules Most Traders Won't Be Able to Follow **118**

The Obvious Rules Are Also the
Most Difficult to Follow... 118

Revenge Trading 119

I Cannot Execute My Stops....................................... 120

So What Is Your "Anti-Edge"? **123**

There Is No Holy Grail to Trading Success **124**

x

Appendix A 127

"Flash Boys": The Book on HFT
by Michael Lewis 127

Appendix B 130

In Publishing and Investing,
the Little Guy Never Had It so Good 130

Acknowledgements 132

References 133

About the Author 142

Index 143

Chapter 1

Treacherous Markets

Introduction

Another book on the financial markets that is about to reveal the Holy Grail to endless profits? Not quite.

Today, a great number of individuals, from workers to savers to retirees, have some exposure to the markets. For most of these individuals this exposure is an indirect one, with their monies managed by mutual funds, pension funds, insurance companies and the like. If you include the sovereign wealth funds (government investment funds), then you can add on many more millions of citizens who are also indirect investors. However the focus of this book is not these individuals but rather the do-it-yourself individual investor-trader, trading through her own brokerage account. While the latter variety of individual investor has diminished in number quite dramatically over recent decades, there are still many of us who prefer to manage at least a part of our investments.

After trading and constantly thinking about the markets for the past forty years, with twenty of those years spent first as a broker and then a Local, I have come to realize that there is so much about the markets that is rarely discussed outside the financial services community. These are issues that are terribly important to the financial well-being of individual investors and deserve much greater coverage. It is my hope that this book makes a meaningful contribution towards this effort.

> ## By the Way, What Is a Local?
> A Local is a class of trader, often described as a profes-sional scalper, on a derivatives exchange. Typically an individual, the Local can trade only for his own account. In exchange for providing liquidity, the Local enjoys lower transaction costs on his trades. The activities, obligations, and privileges of a Local may differ from one jurisdiction to another.

I have endeavored to write this book in language that is accessi-ble to the novice trader-investor. The idea is that you enjoy the read while you learn new ways of interacting with the markets, fully aware of the changes happening around you. Learn about the important events and developments, especially develop-ments in trading technologies, that have transformed the mar-kets, particularly over the past decade. I discuss, at length, the issue of High Frequency Trading (HFT) in an attempt to give you a clearer picture of the facts minus the hype.

Individual Investor Participation
"Playing the market is the hardest way to make an easy living." This remark comes courtesy of Edward Allen Toppel in "Zen in the Markets"[1]. I like it because so many people are tempted into believing that making a living through trading is easy. And worse still, there are just too many crooks out there who are only too happy to propagate this fallacy.

What really annoys me are the advertisements that promise "big profits for only minutes of work per day". You see these dubious adverts everywhere. Not just on the Internet, where they are to be expected, but in your local dailies and even in mailings from your bank! Most of us are experienced enough to know that such claims simply represent false advertising, and are left flabbergasted as to why nothing is done to stop them. And yet, business must be good, because they keep coming which means they must be roping in enough gullible people.

Despite the best efforts of these con artists, all the evidence points to decreased participation by individuals in markets, especially stock markets, globally. There must be a reason why this is happening despite many markets making new historic highs. The individual investors' faith in the markets was crushed by the financial crisis of 2007/08 and to this day, the perceived ethical disarray that pervades most financial markets is still an issue for many investors.

The heydays of the 1990s and early 2000s when individual investors flocked to stock markets globally are well and truly over.

Jim Cramer, former hedge fund manager and host of CNBC's Mad Money is one of the most recognized faces on business TV. Like him or not, it's difficult to ignore him. Cramer recently (on CNBC, January 15, 2014) talked about his book promotional tour and the kind of reaction he got from people. He says, "People hate the market... the litany of hatred is quite palpable... it's very daunting to talk about the market." He adds, "... what people see is the machines, the machines." More from Cramer, "It doesn't help that every day there is another article about some guy who is being indicted for insider trading...." Anecdotal evidence like this is everywhere and clearly supports the notion that people's faith in the markets has been battered, especially by the issues discussed in this book.

"...what people see is the machines,
the machines.**"**

Among individual participants, short-term traders will suffer the most from today's treacherous markets. There is no denying that even long-term investors will be affected by the changes that markets have experienced in recent years. However my contention is that the negatives are considerably muted for the longer-term investor, especially those trend following investors who hold positions for weeks, months or years.

We begin our look at what drives markets these days by considering the role played by governments and central banks, and then the practice of insider trading. In the following chapters, we take an extended look at the role of machine trading, specifically High Frequency Trading, in shaping today's market environment.

Governments and Central Banks

Intervention by governments in the bond, currency and stock markets has been blatant ever since the Global Financial Crisis of 2007/08. What is good for the financial district will also benefit Main Street, so the logic goes. There are suggestions that similar intervention is active in certain commodity markets as well, in particular the precious metals markets (legitimized by the Gold Reserve Act, 1934, in the U.S.).

The major central banks of the world, the U.S. Federal Reserve, the ECB (European Central Bank) and now the BOJ (Bank of Japan) will ensure that any sign of instability in the financial markets will be smoothed over by a new flood of easy money. Central banks have shown throughout this crisis that they are quite ready to influence markets.

There was a time when even the Chairman of the Federal Reserve, the then much revered Alan Greenspan had limited sway over the markets. On December 5, 1996, Greenspan made his famous "irrational exuberance" remark implying that U.S. stock markets were getting frothy. The market had a minor hiccup then rallied higher for another four plus years until early 2000 when all came crashing down with the bursting of the tech bubble. In those days, central bankers tried to persuade markets through mere talk and were often ignored. Not anymore. Today central bankers and other policy makers drive the markets.

"Abenomics" and State Involvement in the Markets

Central bank independence takes a back seat as Japan brushes aside such niceties to get on with the critical job of mending its economy. After decades of being described as a zombie economy, with anemic growth, deflation, and very high government debt, Prime Minister Shinzō Abe, elected in December 2012, and the newly minted governor of the BOJ Haruhiko Kuroda embarked on a program to fix the economy. This program, or Abenomics as it's come to be known, while including fiscal and structural elements, hinges very much on an aggressive monetary policy involving quantitative easing by the BOJ, a 2 percent inflation target and the weakening of the Japanese currency.

The effect of Abenomics on the stock market has been phenomenal. In 2013, the Nikkei 225 Index rose 57 percent, its biggest gain in 41 years, closing at 16,291. This gain included an immediate jump of almost 1000 points when Kuroda announced monetary stimulus measures on April 4, 2013 that sent "shock and awe" through the markets. The BOJ's measures included increasing its purchases of exchange traded funds (ETFs) and real-estate investment trusts (REITs) giving a direct boost to the stock market.

The weakening Yen has been the primary driver of gains on the Tokyo stock exchange. Abenomics has certainly delivered on its goal of weakening the Yen. In late 2012 about the time of Prime Minister Abe's election, the USD-Yen rate was around 80 Yen to the Dollar. By January 2014, the Yen had weakened to the 105 level. The U.S. Dollar gained 21 percent against the Yen over 2013, its biggest annual gain since 1979.

Happenings in Japan leave little doubt that governments working closely with their central banks are dictating market movements. In the U.S., the Federal Reserve's Quantitative Easing (QE) programs have sent stock prices higher since early 2009 punctuated by declines only during periods when QE was interrupted. The openness with which this is taking place is unprecedented, and frankly a little scary.

How does all this affect the individual investor? Markets that are not driven by economic fundamentals and technical factors but are driven by the dictates of policy makers are inherently dangerous, particularly over the short term. What is a trader to base his investment strategy on? In this environment, charts can be deceiving. Predicting what central banks and governments will do tomorrow may be a fine art that some have mastered, but the average individual investor will be left totally flummoxed.

Even the very long-term, buy-and-hold investor with a 5 to 20 year time horizon has much cause for concern. Who can predict how this era of global monetary easing and potential currency wars will end? Economic historian Marc Faber said in November 2013 that, "Never in the history of mankind have we had universal money printing like now." The consensus among central bankers today is easy money. In this context what former British Prime Minister Margaret Thatcher had to say about consensus seems especially appropriate: "The process of abandoning all beliefs, principles, values, and policies in search of something in which no one believes, but to which no one objects."

The current competitive currency devaluation, post the Global Financial Crisis of 2007/08, has similarities with the trade protectionism of the Great Depression years. Both are attempts to steal an advantage over thy neighbor during a period of global economic distress. The frightening fact is that, after a mega crisis which was the result of over-leverage, only one country in January 2014 is actually attempting to deleverage, and that country is China.

As for Japan's experiment with Abenomics, especially currency devaluation, former Japanese Deputy Finance Minister, Eisuke Sakakibara (popularly known as Mr. Yen) has spoken about his own fears of an *uncontrollable decline* in the Yen. Speaking on CNBC Asia in March, 2013, Sakakibara related how he was "terrified" when the USD-Yen rate weakened to near 150 in

August 1998 while he was still in office, implying that further
weakness in the Yen beyond that level could have been disastrous. George Soros has said as much about the current bout of
deliberate Yen weakening. He talked about how the decline in
the value of the Yen could turn into an "avalanche". Perhaps
the most disturbing commentary came from Lord Adair Turner,
former Chairman of the UK's Financial Services Authority. He
predicted in a speech at the INET (The Institute for New Economic Thinking) conference in Hong Kong in early 2013 that
"Japanese government debt will not be repaid." He went on to
say that it will be monetized, restructured and off-set by high
inflation.

So how is the very long-term, buy-and-hold investor to position
herself? The U.S. and Japan have too much debt. Currency de-
basement cannot go on forever. The benefit the U.S. receives
because the U.S. Dollar is the world's reserve currency, famously described by former French president V. G. d'Estaing as
"The Exorbitant Privilege" won't last forever.

These are treacherous times, and the individual investor has to
tread very carefully.

Insider Trading

Markets have always been plagued by some degree of illegal insider trading. There are numerous examples of anomalous behavior in the prices of stocks or their derivatives immediately
prior to a major announcement.

What Is Insider Trading?

In this book we are concerned with insider trading of the
illegal kind, that is, when someone trades the securities
(stocks, bonds, etc.) of a public company while in posses-

sion of **material nonpublic information**. In the U.S., the principle regulation prohibiting this type of insider trading is the Securities and Exchange Commission (SEC) Rule 10b5-1. For a Hollywood glimpse into the world of insider traders, see Gordon Gekko in action in the 1987 movie "Wall Street".

Insider trading can also refer to the buying or selling of securities by a company insider, like a director or senior management, who does not have unfair access to any information. This is of course perfectly legal. In fact this legal insider trading is considered valuable information and is tracked by many investors.

Very often the options market sees big jumps in activity before major corporate announcements. If you are looking for leverage, the options market is the place to be. So insiders tend to take positions in options before market moving news breaks. If the news is going to be positive for the company's stock price, the insider can profit by purchasing Call options. If the news will be negative, he can buy Put options. The potential profit for the insider can be huge because of the extreme leverage possible with options.

To cite a recent example, on July 12, 2013 AT&T announced a cash takeover bid for LEAP Wireless after the market close. LEAP Wireless Call options were trading record volumes just prior to the announcement. Did someone know something? Writing in TheStreet.com[2], Jon Najarian and David Russell of OptionMonster, review the unusual options activity and point out that, "Those call buyers now stand to make a fortune." They end the article with this poser, "The question now is whether someone will end up in prison for insider trading." Well, based on a complaint, the Options Regulatory Surveillance Authority has deemed it fit to review the option trades.

Incidentally, LEAP Wireless shares closed at $7.98 on Friday, July 12 and opened at $17.23 on July 15, the first trading day after the announcement.

Insider Trading Big Fish

There have been many high-profile insider trading related cases over the years, for example the Ivan Boesky case in the 1980s, to that involving homemaking guru Martha Stewart in the early 2000s. But insider trading cases have taken on a much higher profile of late. This new focus on insider trading coincides with the U.S. government's crackdown which began around the time the financial crisis broke.

Hedge funds and their bosses have featured prominently in the current crackdown. The first big fish to go down was former hedge fund manager Raj Rajaratnam, billionaire founder of the now defunct, New York based hedge fund, The Galleon Group. Rajaratnam, a Sri Lankan Tamil American, was arrested in October 2009 and accused of engaging in insider trading. He stood trial, was found guilty and in October 2011 was sentenced to eleven years in prison.

The Rajaratnam case marked a watershed development in as far as insider trading investigations go: Secret wiretaps were used extensively for the first time. This one development alone sent shock waves through Wall Street. Now any phone conversation a trader might have had could have been monitored. Some of these wiretaps make for fascinating listening, for example, Rajaratnam talking to Danielle Chiesi[3] or the chat between

Rajaratnam and former Goldman Sachs director, Rajat Gupta.[4] (Gupta was himself convicted of insider trading and sentenced to two years in prison. He is free awaiting the outcome of his appeal, at the time of writing. Chiesi was sentenced to thirty months in prison after pleading guilty to securities fraud.)

The next, and ongoing (as of January 2014), public leg of the insider trading investigation by the U.S. authorities would center around hedge fund, SAC Capital Advisors. While Rajaratnam is no small fry, he and his Galleon Group are dwarfed by Steve A. Cohen and SAC Capital, one of the true titans of the hedge fund industry. (Cohen's personal wealth estimated at around $9 billion exceeds the $7 billion under management at Galleon at its peak.)

Not everyone was comfortable with the insider trading related probe on Cohen and SAC Capital. Larry Kudlow, in an episode of CNBC's "The Kudlow Report" (July 19, 2013) asks, "… is this an assault on capitalism?"

SAC Capital, has been described as a "magnet for market cheaters" by Preet Bharara, U.S. Attorney for the Southern District of New York. In July 2013, SAC was charged with "insider trading offenses committed by numerous employees and made possible by institutional practices that encouraged the widespread solicitation and use of illegal inside information." It was alleged that this activity, "resulted in hundreds of millions of dollars in illegal profits and avoided losses at the expense of members of the investing public."[5]

In November 2013, SAC Capital agreed to plead guilty to all counts of the indictment filed in July. It also agreed to pay a $1.2 billion fine and stop managing outside money. The F.B.I. statement[6] on SAC Capital's guilty plea will offer comfort to individual investors concerned about insider trading activity in U.S. markets going forward. April Brooks, a senior F.B.I. official, concluded the statement with these words, "We will relentlessly pursue this anti-competitive criminal behavior until every portfolio manager, every trading desk, every hedge fund owner stops trading on insider information."

To Catch a Trader

Rajaratnam: "OK. How's the market treating you today?"

Adam: "Ah, like a baby treats a diaper."

Snippet of a wiretap involving Raj Rajaratnam. From transcript of Frontline documentary "To Catch a Trader".[7]

To get a feel for how pervasive insider trading actually is, and the massive effort by the U.S. authorities to stamp it out, watch the outstanding documentary from Frontline/PBS, "To Catch a Trader" (54 minutes)[8].

The new found vigor with which the U.S. government is going after insider trading appears to have spread across the Atlantic. The U.K. regulator, the FCA (Financial Conduct Authority, formerly FSA) charged Julian Rifat with eight counts of insider trading in January 2014 after a four year investigation. The case involving Rifat, a former trader at Moore Capital Management LLC, is the U.K.'s biggest insider trading case. There have been twenty-three convictions for insider trading between 2009 and early 2014, with the FCA arresting another fifteen suspects in 2013 alone.

My case in this section on insider trading is to point out to the individual trader that insider trading has actually been quite rampant in recent years. You are at an extreme disadvantage if you are holding a position in a stock in which there is illegal insider activity. What chance does the "little guy" have in an environment where the playing field is heavily tilted in favor of insiders.

Legalize Insider Trading?

Surely the ripple that is developing in this move to legalize insider trading[9] is somebody's idea of a joke. Imagine a world with legalized insider trading where corporate bigwigs will always be at the head of the queue; always buying lower and selling higher than everyone else. More for the 1 percent? I think it's outrageous that such a notion is even entertained and yet it is. Already so many individual investors are abstaining from participating in the markets because of the belief that it's not a level playing field. If ever the individual investor needed a last straw to quit the markets altogether, legalizing insider trading might just be it. The insiders can then have the markets all to themselves.

Chapter 2

The Machines Are Here, Part 1: Introducing Algorithmic Trading, High Frequency Trading

What Is Algorithmic Trading?

If you are looking for a passionate debate on a subject involving the financial markets, look no further that the on-going, raging debate over the positives versus the toxicity of high frequency trading (HFT). High frequency trading rankles a lot of people. To understand why we first need to understand what high frequency trading actually is.

High frequency trading is really a subset, or in other words, one type of algorithmic trading. So what is algorithmic trading then? This is where the fun begins. People can't even agree on a definition for algorithmic trading, let alone HFT. But we'll have to move on, so I am going with the following broad definition of algorithmic trading: Algorithmic trading is any kind of trading that is automated and is based on a decision making process that has been programmed into a computer.

The algorithmic code works with market data to make decisions regarding what to trade, direction, timing, and quantity to buy or sell. The algo system then generates the buy and sell orders typically without any human intervention. Algorithmic trading systems can involve complex programs. If you know any brilliant mathematician who also happens to be a billionaire, chances are he made his money through some form of algorithmic trading.

Within the industry, algorithmic systems are divided into two broad categories. One category is referred to as "execution" algorithms, while the other can be called "decision-making" algorithms. Execution algos are used by funds to dispose of, or acquire large positions without disrupting the market for that security. The best execution algos do their work unnoticed. They are common throughout the world and are among the services offered by major brokerages to their institutional clients.

The real action is with the decision making algos. These algos are in the game to generate profits for the hedge funds or proprietary firms that develop them and then unleash them on the markets. High frequency trading is very much within the realm of decision making algorithmic trading.

If you want to keep it really simple, then just think of algorithmic trading as computer driven, automated trading.

The most profitable hedge fund in the world, Renaissance Technologies, founded by brilliant mathematician James Simons, is entirely driven by algorithmic trading. Renaissance Technologies has staff so outstanding in their fields that the company was once described as having the best math and physics department in the world. In a rare public speech at MIT in

December of 2010[10], Simons gives us a glimpse into the highly secretive world of his quant firm. He talks about how he shifted to a 100 percent computer models based approach to trading after finding the traditional fundamental approach too much of an emotional rollercoaster. Renaissance Technologies' quantitative Medallion Fund which was founded in 1988 was closed to outside investors in 1993, and has been entirely owned by employees since 2005. In the world of algo trading, Simons will always be remembered as a pioneering legend.

For a long time, getting a machine or computer to do your emotionless trading meant a heavy trade-off; you would lose the valuable "feel" for the market that you may possess. Essentially, all the positive elements of discretionary trading would be lost. But not any more apparently. Some of today's trading algorithms are so sophisticated they incorporate artificial intelligence and human psychological or behavioral elements. The best brains in the world are put to work developing highly complex code that drive these frontier-breaking algorithmic trading systems. Young exceptionally brilliant graduates in mathematics, physics and engineering from the best universities are grabbed by the algo outfits.

Despite the advances in algorithmic trading, according to a Bloomberg article[11], quant-based hedge funds have been struggling over the past three years due in part to central bank intervention. "Such interventions in the market can alter the expected movements of securities prices, managers say, leading to losses for the funds," says the report.

What Is High Frequency Trading (HFT)?

As stated above, HFT may be considered a subset of algorithmic trading. Not all Algorithmic trading is HFT, but all HFT is algorithmic. The truth is, no two people seem agreed on how to define HFT. Not that there haven't been attempts. Numerous authorities on the subject have had a go at defining HFT. Even the definition that came out of an effort by the U.S. Commodity Futures Trading Commission (CFTC) did not find general agreement.

My own view is that definitions for HFT are quite irrelevant because HFT is really a *technical method or means* of delivering or implementing strategies. Instead, focus should be on the strategies themselves, including those strategies that are specific to the HFT method.

Think of HFT as always having the following characteristics:

- Very high speed (or low latency)
- Very short-term trading, with no positions held overnight
- Individual trades involving profits, losses and volumes that are very small
- Trading frequency is extremely high
- Typically involves colocation (explained below)

Note: Throughout this book, the acronym **HFT** can refer either to High Frequency Trading or High Frequency Trader, while **HFTs** refers to High Frequency Traders.

Very High Speed (or Low Latency)

Speed is vitally important. Once the HFT firms' powerful, high speed computers have processed the code and generated the orders, every effort is made to get these orders to the trading venues, where buy and sell orders are matched, with minimal delay. Digital communications technology is being pushed to its limits in this need for speed. The latency or delay in moving data from one point to another in a network depends on the medium transmitting that data. Optical fiber cables used to be the top end for high speed transmission of trading data. Communications technology though has moved on with first microwave and now even laser transmission[12] being deployed in the race to zero latency.

Without the appropriate exchange technology, HFT cannot work. This is where people like NASDAQ OMX come in. They are spreading their technology to all corners of the globe making HFT a global phenomenon. Speaking on CNBC Asia in February 2014, Robert Frojd, NASDAQ OMX General Manager of South Asia, SE Asia and Pacific said, "We believe that HFT is already here and we think it's here to stay. And that it's more a question of how much of it the regulators will allow on a country by country basis." All the big HFT firms have offices in Europe and the preferred Asian hub, Singapore.

Very Short-Term, with No Positions Held Overnight

High frequency traders (HFTs) do not hold their positions beyond a maximum of about ten minutes. In fact, the average holding period is measured in seconds or milliseconds (thousandths of a second). They are hyper short-term day traders. Positions are typically not held beyond the more liquid, normal trading hours for fear of event risks.

Individual Trades Involve Profits, Losses and Volumes That Are Very Small

Profits and losses are typically measured in fractions of a cent per unit traded. According to older estimates, the top firms made about 60 percent of the time and lost the same amount about 40 percent of the time. More recent estimates put the winning percentage much lower, just above 50 percent.[13]

Volume per trade is kept low so trading can be nimble. In the main, this activity is classified as market making by HFT proponents and as scalping by critics.

Trading Frequency Is Extremely High

While the profit per trade is small, the volume traded can be extremely high. Depending on the liquidity of the stocks being traded, thousands of trades may be executed per day on just one stock. About half the volume on the world's biggest and most important stock market, the U.S. stock market, is being done by computers, not humans (off a high closer to 70 percent) while in Europe it's 45 percent of all equity trading[14] and in Australia 32 percent by one estimate[15]. Additionally, HFT generates significant volume in other markets, including futures markets and the foreign exchange market.

Typically Involves Colocation

For a lot of people who are unfamiliar with HFT, colocation will seem like an outrageous, almost absurd length to go to for a miniscule speed advantage. But in the world of HFT, no effort is too great to achieve a speed advantage over your rivals. And by speed advantage I mean shaving off milliseconds or microseconds (millionths of a second) from the time it takes an order to travel from the HFT firm's computer to the exchange and back. Again, colocation is all about speed, about reducing latency.

The quickest way to get an order from your computer to that of the exchange would be to physically locate your computer right next to the exchange's computers. This is exactly what colocation accomplishes. Many exchanges throughout the world now offer facilities that allow a HFT firm to place their trading computers in the same building that houses the exchanges' computers. These exchange computers do the work of matching buy and sell orders. They also provide market data feeds to paying clients.

Colocation is available to anyone who wants it. But competition for the limited slots is usually intense, and it is expensive, though costs are coming down all the time. The New York Stock Exchange and the NASDAQ Stock Exchange offer their colocation facilities in sprawling, high-security facilities at different sites in New Jersey. The National Stock Exchange of India, the Singapore Exchange and the Australian Stock Exchange are among numerous exchanges worldwide offering colocation facilities.

The provision of colocation facilities can be a lucrative source of revenue for an exchange. The SGX, the stock exchange of Singapore, advertises its facility in its website as follows:

"SGX Co-Location Service offers you the opportunity to place your systems in the same data centre as SGX mission-critical trading and market data engines. Designed specifically to meet the rigorous demands of global financial institutions, Co-Location provides access to SGX market data and trade execution systems at unparalleled speed."[16]

If you're worried that your firm's colocated server, positioned in a corner of the building furthest away from the exchange's computer will be at a disadvantage to the other more closely colocated servers, do not fear. Most colocation facilities will provide a standard length cable to all client servers so that precise location within the facility is a non-issue. Wow! What more can you ask for.

The Great HFT Debate

High frequency trading is controversial and currently creating a furor among market professionals and the general public. There are entrenched camps, generally with vested interests, vehemently arguing for and against HFT.

To give you a flavor of the intensity of this debate, consider the following remark by Irene Aldridge[17], a strong proponent of HFT, on the views of two well established HFT critics: "Brokers like Arnuk and Saluzzi (2012), for example, denounce automation, yet wax eloquent about those manual error-prone days when investors were not allowed on exchanges and brokers were the fat cats of the world."

On the other side of the debate we have this from Tyler Durden (pseudonym for Dan Ivandjiiski[18]) on the website Zero Hedge, "Everyone knows that the most parasitic form of trading, that would be high frequency trading for those who may not have followed this website since 2009, is very profitable. Well, it is certainly profitable for those who operate the momentum-igniting, quote churning, queue jumping HFT firms in control of what's left of the "market", if not so much for anyone else."[19]

The feuding goes on.

Is HFT Making Markets More Treacherous?

Yes and No. When I first started researching the subject of HFT, I was convinced that HFT was the enemy. It wasn't just the much publicized disruptive aspects of this methodology, exemplified by the quite frightening intraday "Flash Crash" of May 6, 2010 in the U.S. when the Dow Jones Industrial Average fell by almost 1000 points in a matter of minutes (more on this later). It wasn't just that individuals, both professional and part-time, scalpers and day traders were being decimated as the machines moved in. It was an almost instinctive pushback against the perceived "big boyz who were out to kill off the small investor-trader".

On my part, confirmatory bias (the tendency to seek out what reiterates your own views) was in full swing. I kept reading articles, comments, blogs and books, but only those opposed to HFT. Fortunately the scientific process I was taught to appreciate throughout my education was not compromised. The more I read, the more I found my position against HFT increasingly tenuous. I began to realize that the pro-HFT folks weren't just "the lobby" but actually had some really valid arguments in support of their cause. So then I began reading stuff by HFT proponents and more balanced arguments by people like Larry Tabb of the TABB Group[20] and the academic community.

It would appear that the initial broadly negative sentiment towards HFT among market participants, coming on the heels of disruptive events like the Flash Crash, may be waning somewhat. For example, a February 2014 article in POLITICO[21] discusses the changing position of initially critical farm groups as they engage with HFT market makers who are explaining their role in agricultural futures markets.

Today I am of the view that there is both "good" and "bad" HFT. This is a view held by many interested parties, from institutional investors like the Vanguard Group[22], to academics and others[23]. In a March 2014 Reuters article, James Angel, a professor at Georgetown University specializing in financial markets, responded to criticism of certain HFT practices in this way, "Not everyone with a fast computer is a bad guy. Rather than restrict all fast computers, we need regulators who can tell the good from the bad and keep the bad guys out."[24]

Over the next two chapters I will try to make my case, and most importantly describe how HFT affects you, the individual investor/trader. There is a lot of unwarranted hysteria around the subject of HFT. The equation is really quite simple: Guard against bad HFT and take advantage of what good HFT has to offer. The markets are being made more treacherous, but only by bad HFT while good HFT is making it better for all investors, especially longer-term retail investors.

Chapter **3**

The Machines Are Here, Part 2: Into the Guts of HFT

HFT Strategies

As discussed in the previous chapter, HFT is merely a technological advancement that is being utilized to implement certain trading strategies. Most of these strategies have been around for ages and have previously been executed through means other than HFT, while some may be new and specific to HFT. In the following section I describe the common HFT strategies.

Market Making

Market making was an integral part of financial markets even in the days when shares were traded under trees and at street corners. The market maker is a middleman much like your typical used car dealer. The used car dealer buys a car from a seller and then sells it on to a buyer at a higher price. In the financial markets, the difference between the dealer's buying price and selling price is referred to as the "spread". The wider the spread, the greater the profit for the car dealer or the market maker. In this way, sellers don't have to wait around for buyers to turn up and vice versa. This intermediation service offered by market makers is essential to the smooth operation of stock and other asset markets. Market makers provide "liquidity" which allows buyers and sellers to enter and exit immediately and without significantly moving the prevailing price.

Before the days of the electronic exchange, market makers called "specialists" were the middlemen at the New York Stock Exchange (NYSE). Their counterparts at the NASDAQ were called registered market makers or dealers. There was considerable dissatisfaction with the way specialists and registered market makers operated. While these market makers of old had many rules governing their operation, they also enjoyed exclusivity and huge profits. Several scandals, especially one involving NASDAQ market makers in the mid-90s, and another involving NYSE specialists between 1999 and 2003, only increased the clamoring for change.

The late 1990s saw the birth of fully electronic trading venues, precursors to fully electronic stock exchanges. The innovators of these digital trading networks were determined to eliminate the traditional market makers. The idea was for end buyers and sellers to deal directly with each other. Alas their noble intentions proved impractical and a new breed of middlemen, the HFT market maker, quickly settled into the role of providing the necessary intermediation service.

Market making is such an important HFT activity that you could even think of HFT strategies as being comprised of formal market making, informal market making and then other strategies. Formal HFT market makers include the likes of KCG Holdings (the merged HFT giant GETCO and Knight Capital), who operate as a designated market maker (DMM) at the NYSE. Informal HFT market makers employ the same strategies but do not have the obligations or enjoy the privileges that come with designation as a formal market maker.

HFT market makers earn their profits from the bid-ask spread and/or from rebates offered by the exchanges to encourage their participation. Exchanges want market makers to partici- pate because they add the much desired liquidity that all ex- changes try to attract. When an HFT market maker works for the rebate offered by an exchange, through what is known as the "maker-taker" pricing model, the HFT is said to be engaged in an activity called "rebate arbitrage".

Relative Value Arbitrage

Next to market making, relative value/statistical arbitrage, or simply arbitrage, is probably the most common HFT strategy. Arbitrage is relatively risk free and fully exploits the speed of HFT. An HFT firm involved in arbitrage can profit from very short lived, tiny miss-alignments in price between correlated securities. For example, the E-Mini S&P 500 futures contract traded on the Chicago Mercantile Exchange has a direct rela- tionship with the SPY exchange traded fund (ETF) which tracks the component stocks of the S&P 500 index. Should the E-Mini contract trade at a price that is high relative to the value of the SPY ETF even for a sub-second, the HFT arbitrageur will sell the E-Mini contract and buy an appropriate amount of the SPY. When prices revert back to their normal relationship, the HFT arbitrageur will unwind his position by buying back the E-Mini contract and selling the SPY, thus locking in his profit. (The arbitrage position can also be unwound on expira- tion of the futures contract.)

Since every HFT firm is constantly on the lookout for arbitrage opportunities, speed is essential for success. Maybe now we can understand why a company would drill through the earth's crust along the shortest route possible to lay straight fiber-optic cables between Chicago and the stock exchange data centers in New Jersey. Incidentally, even as this link was completed, it was surpassed in speed by a new microwave link.

The proliferation of ETFs over the past decade created ample arbitrage opportunities as slight mispricings between ETFs and their underlying constituents occur. Stocks and their corresponding options will also present arbitrage opportunities as will price discrepancies between correlated assets like say the price of crude oil and airline stocks. Then there are also more complex arbitrage situations involving portfolios of stocks.

Arbitrage can also take place on an instrument that trades in more than one location like Apple shares which trade in Frankfurt and New York or the Nikkei 225 futures contract which trades in Singapore and Osaka. (Incidentally, the arbitrage between Osaka and Singapore futures is so seamless, I could actually trade Osaka futures while watching the Singapore futures charts.)

Trend and Event-Based Strategies

These strategies involve taking a directional bet. They have also been referred to as momentum strategies. High frequency traders (HFTs) are characterized by very short-term trend trading, from milliseconds to a maximum of a few minutes. HFT or algorithmic strategies that go beyond a few minutes have been pursued for some time, but the reality suggests that they have yet to make the grade[25]. A computerized Warren Buffet is apparently some ways off, as is an algorithm that can beat a good poker player.

Still, there is ample opportunity for HFT to leverage its speed advantage in the area of event-based, directional trading. Breaking market-sensitive geopolitical, economic or corporate news, now made available in machine readable format, has been exploited by HFTs to trend-trade ahead of the broad market.

Other trend trading strategies include "order anticipation" where the HFTs use their technological edge to anticipate large orders, the so called "whales", and trade ahead of them. For example, using certain strategies, an HFT may detect a disguised, large sell order by a mutual fund. To profit from this information, the HFT will trade in the direction of the order flow, selling first and then buying back its position as the price drops.

Even your innocuous tweets and other public posts are being constantly mined and assessed for market relevance. HFTs have been known to trade off information gleaned from Twitter. A sudden selloff in the stock market on April 23, 2013, an incident called the Hash Crash, resulted from a false twitter feed about an explosion at the White House which came from a hacked Associated Press twitter account.

HFT trend and event-based trading approximates the kind of trading a human day trader might do, except a lot faster. This HFT strategy is obviously much riskier than either market making or arbitrage.

Spoofing, Layering, Momentum Ignition
These strategies have been around since way before the appearance of HFT. They can be implemented by a guy at a keyboard or a low frequency algo as well as HFTs. In all three strategies, the intention is to create a false market that induces the victim

to trade in the direction that profits the perpetrator of the strategy.

In spoofing, an outsized order is placed and canceled quickly at or near the best bid or offer to create an impression of buying or selling pressure. Often the spoofing party already has a position and uses the strategy to exit at a favorable price. Layering is essentially similar to spoofing except that a series of orders are placed leading up to the best bid or offer. In momentum ignition a rapid price move is artificially triggered allowing the instigator to trade out with a profit or enter a favorable position and trade out as prices quickly settle back.

Latency Arbitrage, Quote Stuffing

Both these HFT-specific strategies can be classified as structural HFT strategies in that they are deemed to "exploit structural vulnerabilities in the market or in certain market participants" (compare with reference[26]).

Latency arbitrage is essentially a U.S. issue that has been highlighted by Arnuk and Saluzzi[27]. According to them, some HFTs profit from faster access to market data via colocation and direct data feeds from exchanges. They claim that this allows these HFTs to see and trade quotes in advance of the general public who rely on the slower quotes dissemination system commonly known as the Security Information Processor (SIP).

Quote stuffing is more widely recognized as an HFT strategy than is latency arbitrage. However, there are several explanations, some nefarious others more innocent, as to exactly why HFTs indulge in quote stuffing. The most widely accepted explanation is that HFTs deliberately flood the system with extremely rapid orders and cancelations to "jam up" the network for other participants who don't have the capability to deal with the flood of data. This in turn gives the quote stuffing HFT an unfair informational edge from which it can profit.

HFTs are notorious for their extremely high order cancelation rates. Typically about 90 percent of quotes are canceled.

The Nature and Effects of HFT

Certain strategies can be readily identified as "bad" HFT because they are manipulative or cause market disruptions. Bad HFT only makes today's markets more treacherous and should be neutralized. Other strategies are widely recognized as beneficial and hence classify as "good" HFT.

It would be very convenient if all HFT strategies could be neatly and unambiguously categorized as "good" HFT or "bad" HFT. But clearly this is not the case. Some strategies may be good in one market environment yet bad in another. HFT is controversial because HFT strategies are controversial; some more so than others.

Manipulative HFT

Some HFT strategies are outright nefarious. Manipulative HFT strategies are mostly already illegal and should just be eliminated through enforcement. Spoofing, and the related layering and momentum ignition, plus probably quote stuffing, fall into this category.

For a long time, few people contemplated the possible threat of market manipulation from algorithmic and high frequency trading. The incident that blew the lid of this particular can of worms came in 2009.

Sergei Aleynikov, a Russian immigrant to the U.S. and former Goldman Sachs programmer was accused of improperly copying computer code from a Goldman high frequency trading unit. During the course of the case, Assistant U.S. Attorney Joseph Facciponti said, "The bank has raised the possibility that there is a danger that somebody who knew how to use this program could use it to manipulate markets in unfair ways." This revelation set off alarm bells and permanently changed the way computerized trading would be perceived.

Since then several cases involving spoofing and layering have surfaced. In September 2012 the U.S. Securities and Exchange Commission (SEC) issued a cease-and-desist order against Hold Brothers On-Line Investment Services for manipulative HFT spoofing and layering activities. As Kirilenko and Lo (2013)[28] point out, one example of the manipulative activity took all of 839 milliseconds to accomplish, and in their words, "It is a physical impossibility for any human trader to have accomplished this manually." They then add, "However, their behavior is unlikely to be an isolated incident, which highlights the challenges facing regulators who need to revamp their surveillance and enforcement practices to be effective in catching the cyber-fraudsters of today."

In another case, the U.S. Commodities and Futures Trading Commission (CFTC) in July 2013 ordered Panther Energy Trading LLC and its Principal Michael J. Coscia to Pay $2.8 Million and banned them from trading for 1 year for "spoofing in numerous commodity futures contracts"[29]. The manipulative HFT spoofing involved 18 futures contracts traded on the Chicago Mercantile Exchange Group's Globex online trading platform.

Most retail traders and investors will have come across spoofing and its variants (layering, momentum ignition) at some point in their trading history. While these manipulative strategies have been around way before computerized trading appeared, the difference is that the algos do a better job of it than humans ever did, and the best executors of these strategies are of course the HFTs. Every innovation will bring with it its miscreants.

Individual investors have had to endure these manipulative practices for ages. Yet it is only now, because of the involvement of bad HFT, that such practices are garnering the notoriety and enforcement action they deserve. Better late than never, I guess.

Disruptive HFT

HFT can sometimes either cause or exacerbate disruptive events in the markets.

Disruptive HFT makes the headlines and for good reason. Destabilizing events damage the integrity of markets. They are traumatic, scaring investors away, especially retail investors and something needs to be done to eliminate or at least limit these events. The good news is that something *is* being done about it. (More on this in the next chapter.)

The mother of all HFT-related market disruptions must be the events of May 6, 2010; the incident that has come to be known as the Flash Crash.

The Flash Crash

The Flash Crash, while mainly a U.S. phenomenon, is an essential topic in any discussion of HFT for one reason: It was the event that, with a little help from the media, brought HFT into public focus. Prior to May 6, 2010 few market outsiders knew about HFT.

The impact of the immediate media coverage was to leave the impression among the investing public that the Flash Crash was entirely the doing of HFT. Investigations would later reveal that this was not quite the case.

What Happened

- By 2:30 p.m. on May 6, 2010, due to weakness emanating from problems in Europe, the Dow Jones Industrial Average (DJIA) was down about 3 percent for the day.

- At 2:32 an execution algorithm to sell 75,000 S&P 500 E-Mini futures contracts, valued at about $4.1 Billion, on behalf of a large mutual fund kicked in.

- Then came the cataclysmic *plunge and bounce back, all within about ten minutes*. The collapse starting from 2:41 took the DJIA down an additional 700 points. At the lows the DJIA was down almost 1000 points for the day, equal to a decline of 9.2 percent.

- During the chaotic plunge and recovery, stock prices went crazy. Accenture, the multinational consulting firm, traded at $0.01, down from nearly $40, while Apple shot up to $100,000.

The Flash Crash started with selling activity in the S&P 500 E-Mini futures contract traded on the Chicago Mercantile Exchange (CME). Cross-market arbitrageurs then spread the selling to the equity market via the SPY ETF and eventually individual stocks and other ETFs. The selling frenzy stopped and reversed only when the CME's five second automatic pause, to slow down trading, was triggered in the E-Mini contract. As quickly as they had fallen, the E-Mini futures, equities and options markets all recovered to pre-crash levels.

Regulators eventually ruled that all trades done at more than 60 percent from levels before the crash (the 2:40 p.m. value), would be canceled. More than 20,000 trades in all, at least half of which by share volume were retail orders[30], were canceled as a result. But many trades done at ridiculous prices, a little less than 60 percent from pre-crash levels, were considered good and stood resulting in huge losses for many unlucky investors and of course handsome gains for traders on the other side of those trades.

The investing public was shocked by the extreme volatility exhibited by the markets. Stock market veterans though were immediately reminded of an equally shocking event that took place some twenty-three years earlier—the great crash of October 19, 1987 also known as Black Monday.

Black Monday, October 1987: The Original Flash Crash?

The greatest *one-day* crash in U.S. stock market history was the crash of October 19, 1987 when the Dow Jones Industrial Average (DJIA) fell all of 22.6 percent. The reverberations of this shock event were felt throughout the investing world. Stock markets everywhere, in every nation which had an open economy, were affected.

In the days leading up to Black Monday there already were signs that the stock market was set for a major break. When Asian investors woke up on Saturday morning, October 17, to find that the DJIA had fallen another 108 points in Friday trading, after days of weakness, a distinct sense of panic set in. A crash mindset was firmly in place with traders expecting a bloodbath on Monday.

Few people realize that the big plunge did not start on Wall Street; it actually began in Asia while Wall Street traders were trying, probably without much success, to get some sleep that Sunday night. On a personal note, Black Monday was a career changing experience for me. It taught me that as a trader and investor, one should always be prepared for the unthinkable black swan event.

After major plunges in Asia, led by the Hong Kong stock market (Shanghai and Shenzhen stock exchanges did not yet exist), futures were already trading sharply lower in New York before the stock market open. What happened the rest of that day was essentially computer driven, the result of algorithmic trading, though it was then called program trading and "portfolio insurance". Computer trading did not trigger the crash, but it certainly exacerbated the volatility.

As stocks fell, traders hedged their position by selling futures which in turn resulted in arbitrage selling of stocks and then more futures selling and so on. In essence a feedback loop developed that sent prices crashing ever lower. Without any means of interrupting the momentum of the fall and disrupting the feedback loop, there was no opportunity for genuine buyers to assess fundamental value and step in and buy. (Market-wide circuit breakers were only put in place in 1988 as a result of the Black Monday experience.)

One significant aspect of the Black Monday debacle was the way market makers abandoned their posts. Both NASDAQ market makers, who refused to pick up their phones, and NYSE specialists were overwhelmed by the selling and pulled out of the markets. Survival came first; quotation obligations be damned. In fact, on Tuesday morning, October 20, market makers were heavy sellers as they liquidated inventory they had acquired the previous day accentuating morning selling pressure. "'The specialist system just let {stocks} go. People just stood aside,' says Leslie Quick Jr., the chairman of Quick & Reilly Group Inc., a big discount brokerage firm." (A quote from the excellent Wall Street Journal Article first published on November 20, 1987: "Terrible Tuesday: How the Stock Market Almost Disintegrated A Day After the Crash"[31].)

The Flash Crash Debate

In the immediate aftermath of the Flash Crash, the spotlight was squarely on HFT. To most observers, casual or otherwise, it seemed a foregone conclusion that HFT had caused the Flash Crash. However, detailed investigations of the event by regulators and independent researchers revealed something quite different.

Kirilenko and others, (2011)[32] concluded that HFTs *did not trigger* the Flash Crash. According to the regulators (CFTC-SEC report on the Flash Crash[30]) the incident was triggered by a huge sell order for 75,000 E-Mini futures contracts by a Mutual Fund. But HFTs weren't entirely blameless. It is generally accepted that high-speed trading exacerbated the volatility.

One frequently heard complaint is that HFT market makers abandoned the market during the Flash Crash resulting in a liquidity vacuum which added to the extreme volatility. An often cited example is the HFT firm Tradebot which withdrew from the markets when the DJIA was down about 500 points[33]. Another outfit, Tradeworx, is reported to have executed an instruction on their trading system to just "sell everything, and shutdown"[34]. Apparently these new age market makers weren't willing to stand in the way of a tidal wave of selling in a market situation that was entirely alien to everyone. Could you blame them? Besides the unprecedented volatility, several unknowns kept market participants out, including the possibility of a major fundamental event, the integrity of market data, and the potential for trades to be canceled (broken).

Another favorite grouse is that HFT market makers turned aggressive sellers, competing with sell orders already in the markets. They did this as they rebalanced their positions so as to carry no inventory beyond a few minutes in typical HFT mode.

Since commentators seem to like to write about the Flash Crash in metaphors—airplanes diving and recovering, juggling hot potatoes, etc.—I am going to describe the Flash Crash in the following way: HFT may have been the fuel that exacerbated the Flash Crash but the huge E-Mini sell algorithm was the spark that lit the fire, and there was no suitable fire extinguisher to put out the flames once it got going. Suggesting that we get rid of HFT to prevent another fire, is like suggesting we get rid of gasoline because someone might light a match. Far better to not play with matches around gasoline or, at the minimum, have ready appropriate fire extinguishers (volatility/momentum interrupters or circuit breakers).

Alternatively, imagine someone blaming the Flash Crash on HFT. Then imagine someone in 1987 blaming Black Monday on computer-based trading while saying that Black Monday wouldn't have happened if we didn't have any computer trading at all, like in the good old 60s and 70s. Sounds kinda silly right?

HFT is part of the natural evolution of electronic markets. It's new, a bit like the wild-west, so we need to tame it, find solutions to issues, rather than attempt to wipe it out altogether. This final paragraph in the conclusion of the study by Kirilenko and others (2011)[32] summarizes this position well, "We believe that technological innovation is critical for market development.

However, as markets change, appropriate safeguards must be implemented to keep pace with trading practices enabled by advances in technology."

Flash Crash and Black Monday: Differences and Similarities

The Black Monday crash played out over one and a half days in the U.S., while the Flash Crash of May 6, 2010 happened in minutes. Recovery to the old highs took almost 2 years following Black Monday. Black Monday was also a global event affecting markets throughout the world while the Flash Crash was essentially confined to U.S. markets.

While there were differences, the similarities are particularly startling:

- Both events were not triggered but were exacerbated by computer-based trading. Algorithmic program trading and portfolio insurance in 1987 and HFT in 2010. Then NYSE Chairman John J. Phelan's 1987 comment on the role of computer trading during Black Monday as reported in the Wall Street Journal, "The markets will be nothing but an open casino if you let this continue,"[31] sounds eerily similar to the rhetoric following the Flash Crash.

- Cross-market arbitrageurs created a feedback loop between index futures and equities resulting in a cascading effect that sent prices crashing.

- A turnaround in Index futures, the MMI contract in 1987 and E-Mini futures in 2010, sparked the eventual reversal.

- Traditional human market makers in 1987 and modern HFT market makers during the Flash Crash both chose survival over bankruptcy and quit the markets. After the Flash Crash, Chris Concannon of Virtu financial, the giant HFT trading and market making firm, is reported by the Wall Street Journal to have said, "Go back to the 1987 crash, every major firm pulled out."[35]. (Incidentally, the same article states that Virtu continued to trade through the Flash Crash.)

- Market makers turned sellers to shed inventory.
- Both crashes had virtually no impact on the real economy and can be considered entirely market events despite dire predictions especially in 1987.
- Circuit breakers or "volatility/momentum interrupters" were put in place after both incidents to tame the negative effects of technological innovation in the markets.

Money & Speed: Inside the Black Box

A good documentary, published December 13, 2012 on HFT and the Flash Crash is available online. It is titled "Money & Speed: Inside the Black Box" (48:22) (VPRO Backlight)[36]

(Backlight is a series of television documentaries by the VPRO, a Dutch public broadcasting organization.)

Mini Flash Crashes

While these events have come to be called "mini flash crashes", they are really price spikes in either direction, not just down. Typically, an individual stock's price will sprint up or down and then instantly retrace, all within seconds or milliseconds. Wild price moves like these are more than just a bloody nuisance, they can result in investors and traders losing a lot of money.

Among the disruptive HFT events, these may prove to be the biggest thorn in the side of the retail investor.

Because of the availability of the tools to detect disruptive HFT activity like mini flash crashes there is increasing public awareness of these events. There are those who argue that millisecond anomalies in price behavior should not bother anyone. But I disagree. **Retail investors frequently use stop orders**; a fact borne out by the CFTC-SEC final report on the Flash Crash. And these stop orders, used to protect profits or limit losses, can get triggered in a millisecond price spike. Wild swings will force retail investors to either do away with stops, that is, change the way they trade, or to set their stops a lot wider. Either recourse is not satisfactory and may actually result in investors deciding not to trade altogether.

And the SEC is also perturbed by this type of unwanted volatility it would appear. SEC Commissioner Kara Stein pointed out in a speech in New York on February 6, 2014,[37] that mini flash crashes aren't restricted to illiquid stocks. Even heavily traded, global giants like Walmart can fall 5 percent in one second and rebound. But the part of her speech which will resonate most with retail investors is this remark, "While these sharp movements may wreak havoc on the few unlucky investors with outstanding stop-loss orders, so far, they seem to be generally dismissed as inconvenient computer glitches or unwise traders."

Something must be done to limit these wild flash swings, if not eliminate them altogether. The newly instituted Limit Up-Limit Down (LULD) rules will help, but are they enough? I elaborate on the LULD rules in the section titled "Neutralizing Bad HFT" later in this chapter.

There is still much conjecture as to why mini flash crashes occur. Explanations range from good old fashioned gunning of stops to algo glitches or plain human error. There are also more elaborate theories like this one from former HFT insider Haim Bodek (whom you'll read much more about later): According to Bodek, (see[38]) mini flash crashes may be due to HFTs withdrawing quotes and thus creating liquidity pockets in anticipation of sweep events. What this means is that, when HFTs detect a big institutional order that is going to sweep through several levels of orders, they collectively cancel all their quotes leaving a thinned out order book that can result in extreme prices being traded.

Other Disruptions/Glitches

It can be difficult to tell apart routine computer glitches from algos gone awry. Assuming we are not too picky about which of these two possibilities may have been the ultimate cause, then we can just classify this type of event as disruptions/glitches.

The events that come to mind most readily are the Facebook IPO (Initial Public Offering) and BATS Exchange IPO fiascos and the terrifying "Knightmare on Wall Street" (terrifying for Knight Capital shareholders at least).

The IPO of the social media phenomenon Facebook was one of the most anticipated in recent times and had a global audience. Numerous technical glitches on May 18, 2012, the first day of trading of Facebook shares, was not only embarrassing for the NASDAQ exchange on which Facebook was listed, but also resulted in a financial hit for the exchange and investment firms, and losses for investors, especially retail investors[39].

The BATS Global Markets Inc. IPO fiasco borders on the bizarre. The exchange operator was set to go public as the first listing on its own fully electronic exchange, BATS Global Markets, on March 23, 2012. The attempted IPO was hastily aborted after a huge glitch in the exchange's trading platform. Its debut listing crashed from the offer price of $16 to a few cents in a matter of seconds.

The Knight Capital Group was the largest trading firm on Wall Street, churning volume in both NYSE and NASDAQ listed stocks. That was until the morning of August 1, 2012 when a rogue algorithm ran the mighty market maker out of business and eventually into the arms of HFT giant GETCO. The GETCO-Knight Capital merged entity now trades as KCG Holdings. That high speed moment of madness on the morning of August 1, believed to be caused by new market making software that was not properly installed, caused Knight Capital $461 million[40].

There have been numerous other incidents, many likely related to algorithmic trading of one sort or another. Perhaps not very high profile on their own, but taken together, all these incidents have resulted in individual investors becoming quite wary of the markets.

Privileged HFT

HFT firms typically generate high volumes and contribute high fees and are often viewed as privileged clients in this age of for-profit exchanges. Privileged HFT can enjoy certain advantages over other market participants though, importantly, these advantages seem to be diminishing with time.

What I categorize as privileged HFT has been variously described as unfair and discriminatory HFT, abusive HFT, predatory HFT, and so on. But there are also many involved parties who argue that these strategies are perfectly legitimate.

Special Order Types

The use of special order types by HFT came to light only in the first quarter of 2012 although they had been in significant use since 2007[41]. It sparked a major controversy. The man who ignited this controversy was an HFT insider himself, Haim Bodek. Bodek, the founder of Trading Machines, an HFT outfit, turned whistleblower after he realized that certain HFT firms had privileged access to special order types. The special order types gave those HFT firms a distinct edge over their rivals and the rest of the market. As the controversy unfolded it became evident that some stock exchanges, which were all for-profit entities, had been working with their "best clients", meaning those who brought in the most volume, to create custom order types that suited the clients' particular needs. Haim Bodek's story is documented in Scott Patterson's book "Dark Pools"[18]. Bodek later published a book himself, "The Problem of HFT"[42] in which he details the nature of these special order types.

The detailed workings of special order types will be way too complex and mysterious for most of us. For a basic illustration of the *concept* of "queue jumping", I offer the following description: Imagine a situation where you wanted to buy a stock for say $3.50. Before you enter your order, there are already 1000 units bidding to buy at $3.50. Based on the norm of price-time priority, should you enter a standard order to buy 100 shares at $3.50, you will be at the rear of the 1000 units currently queuing. However, it is alleged that using special order types, *in specific situations*, HFTs can violate time priority and get to the front of the queue.

Many HFT strategies, require that the HFT firm always attempt to get its orders to the front of the bid and ask queues. This is why speed is of the essence in HFT. But speed alone is not enough to guarantee first place in the queue. So certain HFTs working with HFT oriented exchanges, devised what basically amounted to order types that allowed their users to *jump the queue*.

This is how Bodek describes it: "The way I think of it is, you walk into your house, you open the front door, and someone's standing in the foyer. You say, 'How did you get there?' and he says, 'I was really fast I ran by you.' No. Actually, you took the back door."[42] Queue jumping is the "special attribute" of one variety of HFT-orientated special order type. There are other special order types that offer their HFT users preferential treatment in different ways.

Bodek and others equally irate over these HFT queue jumping and other shenanigans, argued that either these special order types should be made known to everyone, or they should be eliminated. In this regard, it is worth noting that several exchanges have of late been coming good in terms of fully documenting all available order types and making the documentation easily available. Bodek writes in Chapter 4 of his book "The Problem of HFT", published in January, 2013, "When one reviews market structure changes in the last year, one might note that a number of egregious practices appear to have been eliminated from the exchanges."

Regardless, SEC Commissioner Kara Stein asks in February 2014, "We should try to understand the various order types. Why would one exchange need 80-plus order types?"[37] Industry-wide there are believed to be closer to about 2000 different order types.

There was already a "special order type" creating some controversy before Bodek started his crusade. This was the "flash order". Flash orders were considered unfair because they allowed a group of market participants to get a sub-second peek at certain orders ahead of the rest of the market.

This Is Scary!

From an average investor's perspective, the most troubling aspect of the special order type controversy, is this: For a good five years between 2007 and early 2012, HFTs and electronic exchanges were actively developing and using special order types and profiting from them, while the rest of the industry, including all non-HFT market participants, were totally ignorant of their existence. This is scary! As an individual investor-trader, the participant with the least leverage, it immediately makes me think what else might be going on that I am totally unaware of? The more universal issue here is transparency.

Events-Based Trading

Event-based trading was discussed as one of the basic HFT strategies earlier in this chapter (see Trend and Event-Based Strategies). As pointed out then, HFTs have a distinct speed advantage over the rest of the market which they fully exploit. This speed advantage is not only in executing trades rapidly in response to breaking news, but also in absorbing and interpreting news that is increasingly available in machine-readable format.

Several incidents have put the spotlight on this type of HFT activity creating another area of controversy. The main bone of contention appears to be the fact that HFTs pay for the privilege of receiving information ahead of other market participants and then utilize their speed advantage to trade ahead of everyone else. Critics of this strategy have variously described this practice as unfair, "front running" (usually means trading ahead of client orders) and even a form of insider trading.

New York Attorney General Eric Schneiderman has been particularly concerned with this issue. His office has intervened in at least two cases involving the early release of market moving information to HFTs.

In one case, Thomson Reuters, the multinational media and information firm, was found to be selling early access to the University of Michigan's consumer sentiment survey. HFTs could buy a peek at the data two seconds before the information was released widely. After Schneiderman's office became involved, Reuters said they had decided to stop the early release voluntarily but at the request of the attorney general.[43]

In another case, Berkshire Hathaway owned Business Wire, a press-release distribution company, decided to stop giving HFTs advantageous direct access to corporate announcements. They stopped the controversial practice apparently after both Warren Buffet and Schneiderman's office intervened.[44]

Frankly, I don't see what all the fuss is about. Being the first to react to breaking news has never been a sure way to make money because markets are terribly unpredictable in the way they respond to news, good or bad. (Is good news bad news still or is good news good news now?) Traders who jump in immediately, on breaking economic or corporate news in particular, are really just gambling most of the time.

Special Data Feeds

This is an issue that has been discussed at length by Arnuk and Saluzzi in their book "Broken Markets"[27]. Their argument is that HFTs get access to special direct data feeds that contain enhanced information that only HFTs can use effectively. This information gives the HFTs concerned an unfair advantage over most other market participants, they say. More so, the special data includes stuff that should not be disseminated at all. They make the point that the exchanges see these special data feeds as a source of revenue, or they may provide it for free to their privileged HFT clients as an inducement to trade with that particular exchange.

It should be noted however that these special data feeds are available to anyone who is willing to pay for them.

The Wall Street Code

"The Wall Street Code" (50:29) is another great documentary on HFT published in November 2013 by VPRO Backlight.[45]

(Backlight is a series of television documentaries by the VPRO, a Dutch public broadcasting organization.)

Good HFT

Good HFT is all about market making and arbitrage. Both these activities enhance liquidity, tighten spreads and eventually reduce transaction costs for all investors, according to people who should know, like George Sauter, formerly of the Vanguard Group, the giant fund management company[46].

HFT Arbitrage

HFT arbitrage is virtually controversy-free in that almost everyone is agreed that it is beneficial. High speed relative value arbitrage (or statistical arbitrage) makes markets more efficient. For instance, it's nice to know that the ETF or futures contract you are buying is always accurately priced relative to its underlying components, or that the stock you want to sell is not better priced somewhere else. All the result of silky smooth, instantaneous HFT arbitrage activity.

HFT Market Making

HFT market making, on the other hand, is less universally accepted as good. There clearly are different points of view, but most studies point to the positive, beneficial effects outweighing the negatives[47]. Many studies have shown that HFT market making improves market quality. Increased liquidity, tighter spreads, reduced volatility under normal market conditions, and reduced transaction costs are the usually cited benefits of HFT market making[48,49,50].

The most frequent rebuttal against such HFT-positive studies and reviews is that they are biased, having been conducted by HFT firms, exchanges beholden to HFT firms, or academics sponsored by HFT firms or exchanges[51]. But this criticism clearly does not cover all pro-HFT work. For example see the article by Donefer, "High-Speed Trading Is Progress, Not Piracy"[52] and also the related commentary and update to this commentary[53].

Criticism of HFT Market Making

A lot of the criticism against HFT is actually centered around HFT market making. I list below some of the criticisms which appear with "high frequency" in the literature on HFT market making, and comment on each.

There are essentially three main areas of criticism against HFT market makers: The first relates to obligations, the second to privileges, and the third concerns the tendency of HFT market makers to turn liquidity demanders.

Criticism: The number one complaint against HFT market makers, is that they are not obligated to provide liquidity during times of market stress (like the Flash Crash). They can withdraw their quotes at any time. In fact, formal HFT market makers have minimal obligations to provide quotes at competitive prices (known as affirmative obligation), while informal market makers have no such obligations. This was an even bigger issue in the days before stub quotes (quotes at ridiculous prices like 1 cent or $100,000 which created havoc in the Flash Crash) were banned in late 2010. Traditional market makers were obliged to post competitive prices at all times.

Comment: Soon after the Flash Crash, the big HFT market makers themselves submitted proposals to do away with stub quotes, increase quotation obligations and standardize rules across exchanges.[54] Regardless of this proposal, we must acknowledge that obligations or not, no business entity is going to put its very existence on the line in the face of a violent market turn. The old school market makers ran for cover in 1987. So what do these obligations really mean during periods of extreme stress? As the post-Flash Crash CFTC-SEC Advisory Committee Report put it, "First, even historically, these obligations were of only limited effectiveness during times of extreme volatility because the risks were simply too great."[55]

Expecting heroics from market makers versus creating a free and competitive environment conducive to reestablishing equilibrium in a destabilized market: that seems to be the choice. New measures put in place after the painful "educational experience" of the Flash Crash should work to allow markets to regain stability through natural market forces.

It has been proven that all forms of market makers will renege on their obligations in the face of extreme market moves. Furthermore more obligations come with more privileges and then we have to weigh the benefits of unreliable adherence to obligations against the prospect of the exploitation of exclusive privileges, such as the privilege of seeing customer order flow. Note that during peace time everyone plays by the rules so there are few issues. But it is during periods of extreme stress that things come undone.

The old market makers weren't charitable organizations. They were willing to live with obligations because the spreads made it worth their while! You can't have it both ways, both narrow spreads and obligated market makers.

Several financial economists, going as far back as the 1970s, have periodically proposed a "no obligations, no privileges" form of market making. (cited in the paper by Stanislav Dolgopolov (2013)[56]). So what is happening today is not new at all.

Criticism: HFT market makers have few obligations yet enjoy many privileges. Commonly cited privileges include special order types, special data feeds, and colocation. In essence, they are criticized for having a perceived unfair speed and informational advantage over most other market participants.

Comment: In the section on Privileged HFT I discussed special order types and special data feeds, but did not include colocation or other speed enhancement innovations.

Importantly, if we examine what has been categorized as Privileged HFT, we find privileges or advantages that are all transitory in nature.

Note that special order types are already being neutralized as discussed earlier. Those privileges that are widely considered unfair or discriminatory are already being eliminated.

With regard to the other "privileges" of the HFT market makers, a clear distinction should be made between them and those enjoyed by the traditional market makers: HFT market maker privileges are available to anyone who is willing to pay for them, unlike traditional market maker privileges which were exclusive. In this category we can include special data feeds, colocation and every other speed enhancement innovation.

As long as a privilege is not exclusive, it will tend to be transitory as it becomes more widely available. Even today, it seems anachronistic to go after the speed advantage of HFTs, be it through colocation or ultrafast connections. It's like going after the first traders to use stock ticker machines over telegraph wiring to trade stocks.

As in the case of stock ticker machines, it is just a matter of time before everyone trades through a collocated server either directly or indirectly; it just seems like the most obvious evolutionary path. As many market participants have pointed out, colocation is the fairest way to go because it equalizes the time traders take to access the exchange regardless of the trader's geographic location. (Although it should be noted that the impact of colocation on a particular investor type, retail versus institutional versus HFT, will differ and will also be influenced by the complexity of the market structure.)

The phenomenon of market participants constantly seeking a speed advantage has always been there and will likely continue. In the past, it was "colocated" floor traders jostling for the best spots or brokers wanting to have their phones closest to the trading floor. In the more distant past, those who had the fastest couriers could profit from being the first to receive market moving news from abroad. For a more recent effort at gaining a speed advantage, I can offer the example of screen-based locals (professional scalpers), whom I know, who bought the fastest gaming mouse they could find because they felt it gave them an edge of a few milliseconds.

In the words of Donefer[52], "Speed of information and execution is everyone's objective in the marketplace -- and the current trading infrastructure is no more than a logical extension of a long-term trend."

Criticism: HFT market makers can turn aggressive liquidity demanders and trade with the trend amplifying volatility, especially during periods of market stress. Traditional market makers, who had the privilege of viewing customer order flows, were prevented from destabilizing prices and from front running customer orders (known as negative obligation).

Comment: My contention is that all this does is move price to its equilibrium faster. As long as HFT liquidity taking and trading with the trend does not spiral into a full blown Flash Crash-type event, then all we have is markets behaving the way they will in this age of super-fast everything.

Dark pools (or private stock exchanges whose activities are generally opaque to the public) were started because institutions wanted to escape being scalped by traditional market makers[47], that is, they wanted to avoid negative obligation violation.

The HFT Scalper Model: A Discussion

HFT market making is obviously quite different from the world of traditional market making; from the world of specialists and registered market makers of old. In attempting to describe the activity of HFT market making, or modern market making, some commentators have put forward the idea that HFT market makers actually mimic futures market scalpers in the way they operate.

At the forefront of this proposal is R.T. Leuchtkafer (apparently a pseudonym) who makes a compelling case by drawing parallels between the activities of these two types of market participants. He also points out that some of the pioneering HFT market makers had their origins in the futures pits of Chicago as scalpers or locals[27].

Quoting from the book "Broken Markets" by Arnuk and Saluzzi (2012), this is how Leuchtkafer (who guest authors two chapters) describes these locals or scalpers, "… small-time outfits that made their living rapidly buying and selling futures contracts all day long in the trading pits, making sure never to hold on to any contract for long—studies showed the average holding period was about two minutes—and making sure never to hold positions overnight because they couldn't afford the risk." Sal Arnuk is also an obvious proponent of this idea having made the following remark in a TABB Forum discussion in October 2012, "At some point I am hopeful we will get to the point where we call modern market making what it really is—HFT Scalping."[20]

Having operated as a screen-based local in a futures exchange for five years, I feel compelled to comment on this idea which I will refer to as the HFT Scalper model.

Futures exchanges encouraged locals or scalpers for a reason, and that reason wasn't to earn fees from them which were minimal in most cases. Futures scalpers played a useful role in the markets. Often the viability of a futures contract, whether it could draw other market participants and survive, depended on the degree of activity of scalpers. They provided the immediate liquidity that hedgers, arbitrageurs, and speculators sought. They kept spreads tight and often cushioned sharp moves. If they ever added to volatility it was only when some exogenous event was driving the market in one direction. The futures scalpers themselves could never create the aggressive move minus the exogenous event. The point I want to make in this discussion is this: HFT/modern market making *is* HFT scalping and *there is nothing wrong with that.*

The HFT Scalper model is just a different model, more in keeping with the times. It is an open, competitive, free market model versus the privileged, monopolistic model of the traditional market makers. I believe all efforts should be directed towards creating just such a marketplace, instead of this misguided, vested interest laden effort to stop technological innovation. Adjust to the new paradigm.

Were the futures scalpers successful? Those who acquired the requisite skill-set earned a living with some obviously doing better than others. Those who never got the hang of it, typically dropped out within a year and those who blew up, and lost everything, almost always did so when they decided to take an aggressive directional bet, rather than stick with discipline to the scalping routine of making the spread or just a little more. I believe it is much the same with the HFT scalper model. If the HFT firm sticks with market making and/or arbitrage, then it does consistently well like the Virtu Financials and Tradebots of this world. Once HFTs go into directional trading, there is every chance of them blowing up.

Does the HFT Scalper model inevitably lead to flash crashes? This is where the similarity between futures scalping and HFT scalping stops. Futures scalpers cannot precipitate flash crashes because they are trading a derivative. The underlying cash market will determine price eventually. However HFT scalpers in the stock market are operating in a cash market. And because of cross-market arbitrage, even the stock index futures markets (E-Mini futures etc.) become intertwined with the cash stock market. So, yes, HFT scalpers can precipitate flash crashes, *but only if there are no volatility/momentum interrupters or circuit breakers* (As discussed further in the next chapter on Neutralizing Bad HFT). There is a simple reason why the HFT Scalper model cannot generate flash crashes where there are volatility/momentum interrupters: **no scalper (neither the HFT nor traditional futures variety) will want to have a net position going into a halt.** As a limit price or trading halt approaches, every scalper worth his or her salt, who has been trading in the direction of the trend, will want to get flat. This in itself can cause the market to reverse or at the least decelerate.

If HFT Scalpers were successfully implementing their strategies in the equity markets, they obviously were also going to operate in the birth place of this model, namely the futures markets where screen-based locals like me were still operating. They may have been slow to get to some of the smaller markets, and they may not even have had to be all that high frequency, but they did come eventually and there was no way the human scalper was going to coexist with them. Human scalpers were just out-gunned and displaced. I am one example of a scalper displaced by the machines. And as a good trader always should, I have cut my losses and moved on. Some people are just not able to do this so they linger and try to bring back the good old days.

Equity markets are merely evolving from the specialist/designated market maker model to the HFT scalper/modern market maker model. Is this really a bad thing? No more obligations or privileges. No more fat spreads, high transaction costs, or privileged market access. No more issues with negative obligation violations and abandoning of affirmative obligation in high stress situations. And a better deal for the lowest rung of the equity market food chain, the retail investor. Yes, markets may become more volatile during periods of stress, but as long as things don't go into a full-fledged panic (like in the Flash Crash) then all you get are faster moving markets, which should not bother the longer-term investor too much.

In the conclusion of an academic study titled "High Frequency Trading and Price Discovery" (2013)[50], Brogaard and others say, "When considering the optimal industrial organization of the intermediation sector, HFTs more resembles a highly competitive environment than traditional market structures. A central question is whether there were possible benefits from the old more highly regulated intermediation sector, e.g., requiring continuous liquidity supply and limiting liquidity demand that outweigh lower innovation and higher entry costs typically associated with regulation."

Chapter 4

The Machines Are Here, Part 3: HFT and the Individual Investor

Neutralizing Bad HFT

Any blanket assertion that HFT is negative is off the mark. There clearly are benefits to HFT. There also is "bad" HFT, that is, manipulative and disruptive HFT. If technological innovation is not to be impeded—and I don't think anyone wants that—then bad HFT must be neutralized. Since most innovations bring with them a period of adjustment, I see as quite natural the current phase of having to deal with the misbehaving elements of HFT.

Neutralizing Manipulative HFT

I have already noted a couple of enforcement cases involving obviously manipulative spoofing and layering. With regard to quote stuffing, this is what the regulators had to say in 2010, "In addition, the SEC staff will be working with the market centers in exploring their members' trading practices to identify any unintentional or potentially abusive or manipulative conduct that may cause such system delays that inhibit the ability of market participants to engage in a fair and orderly process of price discovery.[30] Gary Cohn, President of Goldman Sachs, proposed in March 2014 that regulators consider fees on "extreme message traffic" after the approach used in Canada and Australia.[57]

Neutralizing Disruptive HFT

For the retail investor this is an extremely important issue. Disruptive events like the U.S. Flash Crash of 2010, and numerous mini flash crashes over the past several years, have resulted in retail investors suffering significant losses. In the 2010 Flash Crash for instance, a huge proportion of the orders executed at the worst possible prices were retail customer orders (both market orders and stop orders). And while mini flash crashes, which typically last just seconds or less, may seem like only a nuisance, they can cause real damage to retail investors who tend to use stop orders more than other market participants. The stop order, used to contain losses or protect profits, is an integral part of how retail investors manage their trades. If you are anything other than a scalper, meaning if you are even a day trader staring at the screen all day, you will want to use stops. Mental stops are of little use, more so if you are at work, or in Asia and asleep while your stock is trading in the U.S. market. Long-term retail investors who actually shouldn't be monitoring their stocks too closely, will also want to use stop orders.

The problem is mini flash crashes can trigger your stop orders.

Any suggestion that retail investors stop using stop orders is, in my opinion, not a solution at all. The solution should be to *remedy the anomalous price spikes* that trigger stop orders rather than force retail investors to change the way they trade.

Measures to Control Disruptive HFT

A lot of faith is being put on volatility/momentum interrupters or circuit breakers to stop flash crashes and limit the volatility of mini flash crashes.

After the Black Monday incident of 1987, a market-wide circuit breaker was introduced in 1988 which has proven effective in preventing a similar incident. After the Flash Crash, when individual stocks suffered extreme volatility, circuit breakers for individual stocks were quickly put in place. These individual stock circuit breakers have since been replaced by new rules that impose price limits and possible trading halts on individual stocks. Known as the Limit Up-Limit Down (LULD) mechanism, this measure together with a revision to the market-wide circuit breaker are expected to prevent another Flash Crash from happening and put a lid on the volatility of individual stocks during mini flash crash events.

Market-Wide Circuit Breaker and Limit Up-Limit Down (LULD) Explained

In April 2013, a major revision to the market-wide circuit breaker rules from 1988, became effective. The main changes include the use of the S&P 500 index instead of the DJIA to determine threshold levels. Also, the percentage declines that will trigger market halts have been reduced to 7, 13 and 20 percent from 10, 20 and 30 percent previously. The duration of the halt is reduced to 15 minutes instead of 30, 60 and 120 minutes. (If you want more detail, refer to the article "Updating the Market-Wide Circuit Breaker"[58] by Colin Clark and the FAQ by NASDAQ OMX[59].)

Incidentally, during the Flash Crash the prevailing circuit

breaker would have kicked in only if the DJIA declined by about 2150 points (20 percent), way more than the 998 points (9.2 percent) it lost at the lows.

The Limit Up-Limit Down (LULD) mechanism replaced individual stock circuit breakers put in place one year after the Flash Crash. With this more refined measure, each stock will have a dynamically determined upper and lower limit price at any given moment, which together, define a price band for that stock. Under normal conditions, a stock can only trade within this price band. Once a stock's price equals its upper or lower limit price, it is said to be in a "limit state". If it remains in a limit state for 15 seconds, that is, no trades are done (or are possible) away from the limit price for 15 seconds, then trading of the stock is paused for 5 minutes after which it will reopen with an auction.

How are the upper and lower limit prices determined? In very general terms, upper and lower limit prices will be a certain percentage, say 5 or 10 percent above and below the average price of the security over the preceding 5 minutes. Exact percentages will vary from security to security depending essentially on price and liquidity. Details can be found in the FAQ from BATS[60] or the release from NYSE Euronext[61].

As of this writing, LULD seems to be working just fine. Several mini flash crash events have been contained by LULD, as engineered. For example, in a recent case, a price spike in Spectra Energy Corp was capped at 10 percent by LULD without the need for a trading halt.

While retail investors should welcome LULD, there is the problem of limit price levels being too high or too low for some investors. To avoid getting stopped out in a mini flash crash, investors may have to set uncomfortably wide stop levels with their stop orders.

Why Are the LULD Rules and Circuit Breakers Likely to Work?

I can think of several reasons:

LULD and circuit breakers will give market participants the minute pause they require to regain their composure. Investors need time to evaluate prevailing consensus value, and once they do, they will come in to buy or sell. HFT is extremely fast so prices move extremely fast, feedback loops develop, people panic, stops get triggered; all before investors can get a chance to reflect on true consensus value. It happened in 1987 though at a slower pace, and it happened in 2010 at lightning speed. All that was actually needed in both instances was a chance for market participants to just pause so that they could determine that there was no fundamental reason for the fall (a major geo-political event perhaps) and then reflect on consensus valuations. And during the Flash Crash this happened when trading in the E-Mini futures was halted for five seconds.

HFTs are by definition very short term. Now think of what a very short-term trader, *who is aggressively trading with the trend*, would do if she knows that a price limit or trading halt is near or approaching. The very short-term trader would very quickly get flat before that happens because **no HFT or very short-term trader wants to have a net position going into a halt**. So, LULD and circuit breakers will get all the aggressive, liquidity demanding HFTs to go flat as the limit/halt approaches and this in itself can cause the market to reverse or at the least decelerate. There will be competition to cover first and the momentum moves will become more subdued, dampened in amplitude. Eventually the only time you see moves to LULD or market-wide circuit breaker thresholds that trigger trading halts, will be when genuine fundamentals are driving the moves. LULD and circuit breakers may be all the markets need to get back to equilibrium "naturally".

In futures markets, we frequently see pseudo mini flash crashes (price spikes, sometimes extreme) as stops get triggered. And how do market participants react to these events? Human scalpers or traders jump in as quickly as they can to take advantage of the price dislocations. This is likely the fate of HFT mini flash crashes also, only this time it isn't human scalpers jumping in, but other HFTs instead. This will explain why HFT mini flash crashes retrace so rapidly. Now with LULD in place, we could see increased competition to exploit price dislocations and even at levels well before LULD thresholds, thus dampening the price spikes further.

HFT in Decline

The era of the HFT gold-rush is over. Infinium, probably best known for its trading error on the Nymex in 2010, as of this writing, was the most recent casualty in a long list of notable HFT failures.

In fact, the decline was evident in mid-2012 according to a Bloomberg Businessweek article by Matthew Philips, "How the Robots Lost: High-Frequency Trading's Rise and Fall."[62] Quoting estimates from Rosenblatt Securities Inc., Philips lays out some pretty revealing numbers. Between 2008 and 2011, HFT was responsible for up to 66 percent of all trades in the U.S. By 2012, that number had fallen to about 50 percent. The decline in profits was much more pronounced, from $4.9 billion in 2009 to just $810 million in 2012.[63]

Haim Bodek also believes that HFT dominance peaked in 2012.[42] He suggests that the decline of HFT starting in 2012 coincides with a slow cleanup of the HFT industry that began in that year.

The decline in HFT activity and slump in profits since about mid-2012 is probably due to a combination of several factors. Prominent among these would be the fall in market volume, reduced volatility, cannibalizing competition, and the winding down of privileged HFT practices like the use of special order types. Additionally, institutional investors are getting wise to HFT tactics with support from new service providers, and bad HFT practitioners who were also highly profitable, could be phasing out of the markets because of the extreme focus on their activities, on top of enforcement action.

Winners and Losers in the Age of HFT

Any casual observer dropping in on the debate over the merits or demerits of HFT, will likely be overwhelmed by the negative sentiment towards HFT prevailing today. You see it on TV, in the blogs, newspapers, social media, everywhere. It would appear, to the casual observer, that the entire spectrum of market participants, ranging from retail on one end to institutional on the other, see HFT as a menace. Seemingly, the only industry participants benefiting, in other words profiting, from the emergence of HFT are HFT firms themselves and the new electronic exchanges—no one else.

However, a little exploring beyond the discontent, will reveal something quite different.

Institutional Investors

Firstly, institutional investors, your mutual and pension funds, are said to be bleeding from higher costs as a result of "predatory" practices by HFTs. Every time a large institutional order (a "whale" in industry jargon) is in the market, HFTs will sniff it out and front run the order, effectively increasing transaction costs for the fund. Funds, including their mom and pop investors, are said to be clear losers in the age of HFT.

But hold on. If that's the case, then how is it the Vanguard Group, the largest mutual fund company in the U.S., is positive on HFT? George Sauter the former CIO of Vanguard, has been a consistent voice in support of HFT and has often talked about its benefits for investors. He has specifically noted that due to recent innovations in the markets, including HFT, Vanguard has been able to substantially reduce its transaction costs, amounting to "… hundreds of millions of dollars a year in savings to investors in our funds."[46]

Regarding the "predatory" practices mentioned by HFT critics, haven't markets always been predatory? Haven't traders and investors always tried to outwit each other using whatever techniques they could? Is a brilliant tape reader (or screen reader) predatory when he uses his skills to predict the presence of a "whale"? Sounds more like a poor loser wanting to change the rules of the game just because they don't suit him anymore.

But not all institutional traders are poor losers. In fact, most are adapting to the evolving environment and employing new strategies and execution algorithms that can effectively neutralize order anticipating HFTs. Brokers and institutions that refuse to adapt to the changing environment—deploy new tools to serve their clients and investors better—are being left behind. All said, the current situation still seems like an improvement over the days before HFT when many institutional investors used to complain of being front run by intermediaries.

Individual Short-Term Traders

Let's get back to our casual observer. She also notices lots of complaints coming from individual traders. Talk is all about the rise of the machines, about how HFT is pocketing all the profits leaving nothing for the small guy trading independently through his own brokerage account.

If the casual observer listens carefully though, she will notice that most of the complaints are coming from *short-term* traders, not from longer-term investors. And the loudest complaints will be from traditional scalpers, people who have been doing exactly what the HFTs do today. (I should know, I was one of these traditional scalpers.)

Traditional (non-machine) scalpers and even day traders worldwide are being crushed by the machines. And it doesn't have to be HFT that's doing it; low frequency algo trading is formidable enough. Either way, the old school, human, ultra short-term scalper/trader is a loser in the age of HFT.

While some of the affected traders are complaining, others are adapting and shifting to longer time horizons, essentially getting out of the way of the HFTs, as I have done. Here is a typical comment from one such trader, a proprietary trader with Las Vegas based Bright Trading, quoted in the Reuters article "Former stock market 'scalpers' are vocal HFT critics"[64]: "We used to be shorter-term traders, scalpers who were also market makers. Now we're just trading a longer time horizon. You can't come in and expect to scalp."

This is not the first time that scalpers and ultra short-term traders have been displaced by technology. In the recent past, floor traders were forced to switch to screen based trading as exchanges went electronic. Those who could not adapt to the new environment dropped out, but many adjusted and went on to do well. Today's screen-based, short-term trader who is being out-gunned by HFT is no different from the floor trader who was forced out as the trading pits got replaced by electronic exchanges. Short-term strategies deployed by human traders, simply cannot compete with the machines.

Anachronistic intermediaries, slow-to-adapt institutional investors, traditional scalpers and other very short-term individual traders are the only real losers in the age of HFT.

Innovation typically means winners and losers. The losers are complaining.

Retail Investors Are Winners in the Age of HFT

No one needs bad HFT; the manipulative HFT, the flash crashes—big and mini, queue jumping or quote stuffing. And bad HFT is being neutralized. For the longer-term retail investor, using limit orders and executing through a broker with fixed brokerage, I see only positives coming from the new breed of HFT market makers and arbitrageurs: More efficient and liquid markets, narrow spreads, lower transaction costs, and easier, faster market access. The often cited smaller trade size in today's market is obviously not an issue for retail investors who want to trade hundreds or even a few thousand shares.

You may argue that some of these benefits have nothing to do with HFT, but are the result of electronic exchanges or decimalization or something else. The fact is that HFT has promoted and accelerated these innovations with the end result being the electronic marketplace we have today.

The retail investor was a lot more of an outsider, and short-changed as a result, in the days of floor trading compared to the days of electronic trading. And now there is every reason for optimism that she will again be a beneficiary as markets settle into this new era of HFT-dominated electronic markets. All major technological changes will need a period of adjustment as regulators come to grips with the technology, crooks among the early adopters are weeded out, and kinks in the technology are ironed out.

Disciplined, longer-term retail investors are not complaining about HFT.

Leveling the Playing Field—What a Novel Concept!

Something really curious is happening in the age of HFT. There seems to be a sudden, passionate, outpouring of interest in a "level playing field". Now this is definitely a good thing; a level playing field in the markets is always desirable. But this phenomenon has left the retail investor/trader quite flummoxed: When was there ever a level playing field?

Even the most naïve individual investor has always known that it was never a level playing field in the markets. The asymmetries were always there. Retail was always at a disadvantage when it came to costs, information, and speed. Where were these advocates of a level playing field during all those decades when institutional investors were calling the shots and retail was on the losing end?

There has always been a multi-tier market, preferential treatment for certain participants. For example, for decades, in many
countries, proprietary brokerage research was first issued to
institutional investors before release to the public. But one did
not hear much about it and no one really kicked up a fuss. This
has been the case even where retail contributes the bulk of the
commissions as in many emerging markets.

When it comes to speed, again the retail investor/trader has
never been able to compete. If you ever thought that you had a
speed advantage before and incorporated speed to market data
or speed of execution as part of your strategy, you were fooling
yourself and losing money in the process.

So what has changed with the emergence of HFT? Why the
clamoring for a level playing field now? Retail never had the
resources to mount a fight-back against existing asymmetries,
but in the age of HFT, old school brokers and their institutional
clients are clearly fighting back.

It seems to me that the only thing that has changed from the
perspective of the retail investor/trader is that the playing field
which was heavily tilted in favor of the big funds, is now still
tilted against the retail investor—but at a significantly reduced
gradient.

HFT and Individual Investor Confidence

There can be no denying that investor confidence was badly
damaged by the trauma of the Flash Crash, by the canceled
trades, by the trades that stood although done at ridiculous prices. But note that this represented a plunge in investor confidence in an environment of already declining confidence. The
recovery in investor confidence from the Flash Crash would

come with time as it did after the crash of 1987, but unlike then, investor confidence will likely resume its underlying slide.

Note that the decline in retail participation in equity markets has been a global phenomenon most likely more linked to the global financial crisis than the U.S. Flash Crash or baby boomer issues. The Investment Company Institute (ICI) data shows[65] that withdrawals from mutual funds is a trend that started way before the Flash Crash. Investor confidence was crushed by the financial crisis. And despite the efforts of policy makers to support stock markets the world over, that shattered confidence has never been fully repaired. In fact, some investors view the current uptrend as artificial, engineered, and will not participate until free market forces, rather than intervention from governments and central banks, are allowed to dictate how markets behave. Add the continuous stream of insider trading cases, and what we have is a deadly mix that can sap the confidence of any investor. My point is that there are several issues, not only manipulative and disruptive HFT, that must be blamed for the current decline in investor confidence.

Things About Machine Trading That Bother the Average Investor

How Can HFTs Make Money Every Day?

The founder of Tradebot, a Kansas City based HFT firm, said in 2008 that his firm had gone four years without a single losing day.[34] Virtu Financial reported just one losing day from the start of 2009 to the end of 2013, a period spanning 1,238 trading days.[66] Regular folks, even Attorneys General apparently[67], get quite upset when they hear of HFT firms that never have a losing day in years.

The consistently profitable HFTs are electronic market makers and arbitrage outfits that don't take on much risk. What they do is not really trading as it is commonly understood. They provide arbitrage and intermediation services. They are not directional traders. If they were directional traders then they could lose big. Nick Leeson, who single-handedly destroyed Barings Bank, will always be a stark reminder of what can happen when an arbitrageur turns into a directional trader.

Traditional market making in its heyday was good work if you could get it. Specialist firms on the NYSE were known to be very profitable. Old school market makers have even become billionaires, yet no one complained.

During that period when I was a scalper, I never considered what I did to be trading. I went in to work every day, did my "job" and then counted the "wage" I earned at the end of the month. But it was not trading like when I took a position and held in for days, weeks or months. There was always talk about certain scalpers who never had a single losing day, but most successful scalpers would still have losing days, though not often.

With the Machines Taking Over, the Average Investor Has No Chance!
Step out of the whirlpool and the waters will be a lot calmer.

If you step back and look at the broader trends, then all the HFT frenzy will be merely a distraction. Focus on the big picture which will continue to be driven by the fundamentals of the global and domestic economies, company profits, etc. This bigger picture will be reflected in the trend on charts no matter how hard the bots may try to distort the short term. Retail investors need not be phased out of the markets. All they need to do is change their time horizon. Leave the short term to the machines and their algos.

We may be at the cusp of a significant change in investor behavior. Individuals may begin to abandon day trading and other short-term strategies and go back to basics, that is, invest in companies that are making profits, paying dividends and all those other good old fashioned stuff.

Any party that is interested in the well-being of the markets, must protect the interests of the constituency that comprises the individual investor. The alternative may be markets where only state controlled money is put to work financing new companies and growing businesses.

HFT Is like Bacteria

HFT is like bacteria. There is good bacteria and bad bacteria but it's the bad bacteria that's always in the public consciousness. Good HFT, like good bacteria is important and inconspicuously working in the background to keep things running smoothly, to retain general good health. Bad HFT, like bad bacteria can cause the host to become sick and malfunction. Its effects are a lot more dramatic. The goal must be to find a prescription that will get rid of the bad HFT or contain it without killing off the good.

In Summary: Treacherous but Navigable

The mainstream media is on a roll demonizing HFT. Hardly a day goes by without some kind of negative coverage of HFT. Even the twitter sphere is dominated by the anti-HFT "activists" though of late the pro-HFT camp has put in a combative showing. I strongly believe that retail investors must stop and think about how HFT affects them specifically, not how it affects slow-to-adapt institutional investors, or anachronistic brokers and humans employing traditional scalping or other short-term trading strategies. Non-machine short-term trading is out. Go with the natural evolution of the markets, with electronic exchanges and their HFT market makers and arbitrageurs, with efficient pricing, cheap and instant access, tighter spreads, and ready liquidity. There is no stopping technological innovation in the markets. Instead of attempting to kill off HFT, all these clever minds would be put to better use if they just tried to get it to work better.

Yet at the same time do not ignore the dangers. After all, this book is about *navigating* today's *treacherous* markets. Be on the guard for flash events, major and mini, until regulator and industry efforts to eliminate, or at the very least contain these disruptive events, are solidly proven. Today's markets are treacherous, but do not be frightened off. Individual investors represent a vital constituency among market participants. We should take heart from the aggressive global action against insider trading and the taming of bad HFT. Invest for the longer term; make your money work for you. **Today's markets may be treacherous, but they are navigable.**

Note: Please see Appendix A: "Flash Boys": The Book on HFT by Michael Lewis

Chapter 5

Individual Investors Navigating Today's Markets

Introduction

This book revolves around one central theme: That markets have changed, particularly over the past decade; a realization that I hope I have managed to articulate in the preceding chapters. Today's markets may be treacherous, with unpredictable policy-maker intervention, insider trading, and "bad" HFT. But there have also been positive developments for the retail investor like "good" HFT and increased enforcement against illegal insider trading. So what should be the most appropriate response from the average investor?

Think of the mom and pop grocery store you used to know. They have mostly been overrun by the hypermarkets. The same thing is happening in the financial markets except replace the neighborhood grocer with the individual trader. Unlike the small grocer, however, retail financial traders have an option still open to them. Just avoid the "hyper-traders" in the domain where they thrive and move to longer-term investing where they have less of an advantage. Yes, I'm talking good old fashioned, major trend following or whatever other strategy you may fancy, as long as it does not involve very short timeframes; and that definitely includes day trading.

Look, do you expect to ever be in a tennis tournament coming up against Rafael Nadal or Roger Federer? Do you expect to ever jump into a formula one car and deuce it out with Sebastian Vettel or Lewis Hamilton? So why are you willing to compete in the same arena as the professionals when it comes to trading the markets? These professionals have huge human and financial resources at their disposal. Nowhere except in the financial markets do you find so many amateurs competing with professionals in the same arena. Oddly enough, new traders prefer the shorter timeframes initially, but fortunately as they gain more experience most traders tend to gravitate towards longer-term position trading.

"Nowhere except in the financial markets do you find so many amateurs competing with professionals in the same arena."

Individual traders should shift to longer time horizons, but significantly, this shift will be difficult because of all the interests aligned against you doing it. Quick-fire trading, which means higher volumes, benefits virtually the entire financial services industry. Online retail brokerages with their slick trading platforms, live streaming quotes, real-time charting, live news feeds, and volume discounts will have you clicking away with wild abandon. They give you twenty-four hour access to the instrument you trade, always beckoning you to just do something!

Someone is getting richer, and it most definitely isn't you. We're still looking for those elusive customers' yachts.

Time frames are getting shorter and shorter. Traders need to be doing something all the time. Some estimates show that the average holding period for stocks was about four years immediately after the Second World War. Now, if you include HFT activity, the average holding period is likely to be in the minutes.

If you are reading this book looking for market secrets, then this is the single most important "secret" that I have to offer. There are other valuable insights that will help you grow into a consistently profitable investor, but this in my opinion is the first, most important step you need to take to ensure your financial well-being as an individual investor—avoid short-term trading.

Longer-Term Investing Is Where You Should Be

Long-term investing can mean different things to different people. I have to this point, deliberately avoided using the expression buy-and-hold investing. This is because, to me, buy-and-hold implies not only a very long time horizon, say 5 to 20 years, but also a certain inflexibility and passiveness in your investment strategy that I really do not advocate. Long-term investing need not be passive investing and certainly need not involve holding periods as long as five years or more.

Learn to invest like a sovereign wealth fund or a Warren Buffet but at the same time retain the nimbleness that is your advantage as an individual investor. Big long-term investors are like super tankers or fully loaded freight trains; they need time to change course or speed. You, as a relatively small investor can accumulate and distribute your positions without causing even a ripple. My interpretation of long-term investing *does not* imply holding your investments through the rollercoaster of multiple bull and bear market cycles that buy-and-hold investors may be willing to endure. Investing involving the timing of major trends and avoiding the type of frenetic trading that typifies day trading, is probably best suited to the individual investor.

Whatever long-term investing may mean to you, always stick to the instruments you are familiar with. For most individuals these are typically stocks, ETFs, bonds, the more visible commodities like energy, grains and precious metals, and increasingly currency (forex) trading as well.

Long-term investing certainly does not come with any guarantee of profits. Even the most informed long-term investors can still get it terribly wrong. Several sovereign wealth funds, for example, got it spectacularly wrong when they were heavily invested in U.S. financial institutions going into the financial crisis of 2007/08. But as is typical of long-term investing, they have since recovered nicely.

Advantages of investing long term:

- In this age of algorithmic trading and HFT, it is virtually impossible for the human day trader or scalper to beat the machines and succeed. But when you invest longer term, you enjoy all the benefits that HFT brings to the markets, especially for the retail investor.
- You don't need to be a full-time trader. It usually takes years, often as many as ten years before a full-time, short-term trader is consistently profitable. If you don't

believe me ask Al Brooks, well-known ophthalmologist-turned-independent trader, trading coach and author[68]. Are you sufficiently capitalized to survive ten years without any income?

- Psychologically less demanding on the individual. Less stressful.

- The advantages of the professional trader are neutralized when you hold your positions long term. It has never been a level playing field for the "little guy" and it likely never will be. But things are a whole lot better today. When you trade longer term you reduce the gradient of the tilted playing field even more.

- When it comes to reading the macro picture, which is mostly what long-term investing is about, you probably have as much of a chance of getting it right as anyone else, including institutional investors.

- If you have faith in any institution or investor, you can piggyback on their positions. You will obviously be a bit late in your entries, but over the long term it won't really matter.

- Tax benefits to investing longer term in certain countries.

As a long-term investor, you won't be mesmerized by the intraday or even daily gyrations of the markets. Instead, you can always subscribe to the many free, end-of-day charting websites, and your base chart will likely be a daily or weekly chart. By that I mean you should ignore the short-term fluctuations in the instrument you are watching but concern yourself more with how it behaves from week to week. Technical indicators on a weekly chart, like moving averages, are generally more reliable than the same on short-term charts.

Learn to play great defense, not offence, especially during your early years (yes I did mean years) in the markets. Aggressive trading or investing can come later.

In the final analysis, being a long-term investor who only takes long positions (as opposed to short positions), puts you in a stronger position to compete with the big boys.

Shorting Is Not for the Majority

Most individual investors should restrict themselves to trading only from the *long side*, that is buying an instrument hoping to benefit from a price increase. And this is a good thing. Shorting any kind of instrument, that is hoping to benefit from a price decline, is an activity best left to full-time, professional traders. Entirely different, and I would argue more demanding, skills are required when going short.

It helps that you only need to understand the dynamics of markets that are in up trends rather than having to understand markets that are trending up as well as trending down. Some traders love to play the short side because down moves are often much more rapid than up moves. If you are thinking that you will be missing out on the excitement of crashing or plunging markets by sticking to long positions only, you are right. But you are not in the markets for the excitement; profit should be your only motivation.

Most traders will quickly realize that trading the short side profitably can be a lot more difficult than trading the long side. If you find it difficult to ride a winning long position (that is, not sell early as price rises), just know that riding a short position is very much more difficult. The most powerful rallies (short-term price increases) are not seen in bull markets, but in bear markets where they are fuelled by short covering. These short covering rallies can be vicious, causing much pain and shaking out most shorts.

Shorting and Short Covering Rallies Explained

If you are short a particular instrument, say a stock index futures contract like the S&P 500 E-Mini futures, this means that you have sold with the intention of buying back at a lower price. For example, you may have sold 1 lot of the futures contract at the 1800-point level with a target to buy it back at 1750 points. If your trade is successful, then you stand to make 50 points which translates to $2500 going by this particular product's contract specifications. (Instead of a futures contract, you could have sold a stock short, provided you have access to stock borrowing and lending facilities.)

Should the market rise above the level at which you sold short, (1800 in the above example) then your short position will show an unrealized loss in your account. For the E-Mini futures example, with every 1 point gain in the futures contract above 1800, you will see a $50 loss.

As such, when a declining trend reverses and the market starts to rise, traders who have short positions will rush to close their positions by buying back the contract so as to lock in a profit or minimize their losses. This type of buying will produce a **short covering rally**. Note that short covering is not the only buying taking place since other traders will jump on the rally and take fresh long positions intending to profit from the price rise, further fueling the rally.

If you are in the stock market, shorting is more difficult than going long because markets have an inherent bullish bias. Almost all stakeholders, from governments, to major shareholders, to brokers, market operators, and the general investing public want the stock market to go up. The only people who want it to go down are the people holding short positions either in the stocks themselves or in some derivative.

The financial crisis demonstrated that governments won't hesitate to ban short selling to prop up stocks. In September 2008, many traders holding short positions in U.S. financial stocks were decimated when the authorities suddenly banned the short selling of those stocks. Several European countries also banned short selling at the height of the financial crisis. The message here is that should things get really, really bad as opposed to only really bad, the short positions that you are supposed to profit from may do just the opposite and cause you huge losses.

So what do you do when none of the markets you are familiar with are trending up? Well, there is such a thing as not doing anything. Take a break from the markets. Give your nerves a well-deserved rest as you prepare for your next investment once conditions become just right again.

Patiently Wait for the Bull

Most individual investors who have made decent money have done it in a major, persistent uptrend in the stock market, or in other words a bull market. A bull market in stocks is the most fertile ground in which to earn a profit for relatively inexperienced individuals with limited resources. Now, these are the environments in which, as the saying goes, even fools can seem like geniuses.

Bull markets draw in speculators and investors from among the general public. Many will be first-time investors, increasing market volumes and creating an investment environment that offers you a better chance of success, provided you remain disciplined.

It is thus no surprise that most of the truly tried and tested investment methods for individual investors all require a prevailing bull market. In general, all these strategies incorporate some or most of the following elements:

- A prevailing bullish stock market with massive and diversified participation by individuals and institutions.
- Buying stocks that are on the radar of the masses.
- Buying stocks that show or are anticipated to show improving fundamentals.
- Specializing in a few stocks and tracking them closely.
- Buying the strongest stocks immediately after they have consolidated and are breaking out again on rising volume preferably to new highs. (Often these stocks will come back to test the consolidation zone before really taking off.)
- Buying only stocks that hold up well when the broader market undergoes a correction.
- Avoiding stocks that have been market leaders in previous bull markets.
- Keep a hawk's eye on the broad market. When it turns, be prepared to get out.
- Use an exit strategy that incorporates a trailing stop that is based on technical factors or a percentage decline from the high.

These are broad guidelines only that you should research further through reading other books that focus on investment strategies.

The sheer momentum of a bull market and the fact that there are so many "greater fools" participating, means that even the most obvious of strategies can turn a profit. Bull market momentum trading was at its height in the great tech bubble that burst in early 2000. I remember one colorful commentary from that period, "The fools are dancing while the greater fools are watching." Overly optimistic of course, but those on the sidelines sure felt like the greater fools… for as long as the bull market lasted.

In a raging bull market, buying too high is not the problem; it is the *fear* of buying too high that is the problem. The mantra that works best is "buy high, sell higher." And remember that bull markets don't end on bad news, they typically end on good news.

Bull markets eventually come to an end, and all the over-night geniuses will quietly disappear back into the woodwork. Unfortunately, most of the individuals who made money in the bull market, many of them first-time speculators, will then proceed to give back everything they have made, and then some, as they hope in vain for the market to rebound and resume the bull trend. But this is not an unavoidable fate. Mastering the rules of the master traders and applying your strategies with discipline can help you keep your profits as you wait for the next major uptrend to develop.

Chapter **6**

Rules of the Master Traders

Introducing Trading Rules

Executing a profitable trade is difficult. Being a *consistently* profitable trader is much more difficult. While this is clearly the case for short-term trading today as I have stressed in earlier chapters, it is also true for longer-term investing. I firmly believe that individuals are better off investing rather than trading short-term where they are in direct contest with professionals. With this theme as a backdrop, I will discuss in this chapter many of the trading rules that I have learned and applied in my almost forty years in the markets as both a short-term trader (previously) and an investor. Some of the trading rules are more suited to short-term trading but there are also many that are more specific to investing. If you have decided to take a longer term, investment approach to your participation in the financial markets as I advocate, then you should focus on the latter.

Some of the most popular books on trading and investing are essentially books about trading rules. Take the "Market Wizards" series by Jack Schwager[71,72]; the excellent first two books on interviews with top traders are now widely considered trading and investment classics. Yet if you break these books down to their basics, you will find that they are essentially collections of the trading rules applied by the top traders interviewed by Schwager. Even the must-read "Reminiscences of a Stock Operator"[73] by Edwin Lefevre, first published in 1923, based on the life of legendary trader Jesse Livermore, is a collection of the trading rules that Livermore lived by. The list of books covering trading rules is long and I must admit to having a personal liking for them with many in my collection.

Why do so many of us enjoy reading books on trading rules? Most people find it easier to exercise discipline if their possible actions can be whittled down to a set of rules. Even if you are a discretionary trader or investor, as I have been all my life, you still want to "automate" or "make non-discretionary" as much of your trading as possible. In other words, you want to limit the options open to you. You want to keep the decision making, the discretionary part of your trading and investing, to a minimum.

After reading through the rules below, you may end up saying, "But nothing here is really new. It has all been written about before?" Well, you may be right, though I like to think that some of the rules I discuss here are either original or presented in a new light. The focus of this book is clearly the individual investor, particularly new and intermediate level participants. More important than the originality or otherwise of the material presented, is the fact that all the issues raised are important and need to be, not just consumed, but actually practiced. Reading and re-reading the important rules will eventually ingrain them in your psyche to the extent that they become intuitive. When you reach the point where you can honestly declare that you have no more need for books like this, it signals that you have progressed to the level we all strive for—that of the disciplined, rule-following, consistently profitable trader. Then no market will be too treacherous for you to navigate profitably.

The trading rules that follow are mostly my favorites. They are biased towards trading psychology. Developing a trading system that gives you an edge in the markets is important for sure but probably not as important as mastering the psychological aspects of trading. This is certainly not an exhaustive list of all trading rules. And not all popular trading rules are to be followed blindly. I discuss some of these questionable trading rules below. Finally, I point out those very important trading rules that tend to snare most traders. These are the rules you know very well, but are just unable to follow consistently.

Trading Rules to Live By

1. Chill but Never Freeze
When the market is going against you and your stop order is just a few ticks away from being triggered, or the market is surging higher but not yet hitting your target, you will need to muster all the calm your nerves can handle. You need to chill.

Being calm does not mean being frozen into inactivity when action is required. You do not want to become like the proverbial "deer in the headlights", frozen, paralyzed by fear. Always be prepared to act. Say the market opens gap down plunging through your stop-loss levels (i.e. price levels at which you have decided you will cut your losses); what do you do? You should already have a plan for just such an eventuality, and then simply execute the plan. Remember, your stop-loss level is not negotiable. If you freeze in a fast moving market, you can do your account irreparable damage.

2. Poker Principles

Long before I started trading, I used to play poker (a variant of five-card stud) with family and friends on a regular basis. I was consistently successful. And while I did not realize it then, I was actually working with a set of rules that I had developed intuitively over the years. One day, after I had been trading for awhile, I sat down and wrote out the rules I used to follow when I played poker. I came to call these rules the "poker principles" and it was immediately evident that these same rules could be applied to trading the markets.

Poker and Trading

If you are not convinced about the parallel between trading and poker, examine the infographic by tradimo.com, "A Comparison of Traders & Poker Players"[74].

For more on the similarities between poker and trading, watch Bloomberg TV's special feature Poker Night on Wall Street (video, 44 minutes)[75] aired on October 23, 2013. Hosted by Trish Regan, the poker game had 6 Wall Street titans in the mix, among them Jim Chanos, David Einhorn and Mario Gabelli. According to Regan in her introduction, "It's the game every banker, broker and trader wants to master. Poker is Wall Street's newest obsession. The parallels between smart investing strategy and killer poker moves can't be denied."

My poker principles were:

1. To win you must play determined to win, and concentrate fully.
    (In other words, no fooling around, drinking a lot of

beer and enjoying the company rather than focusing on the game.)

2. Always play a solitary game. (More on this below.)
3. If the cards you are played are bad, close quickly and lose little. (Be patient and wait for the best signals or setups. Cut your losses short.)
4. Pile in when cards are good. (More on this below.)
5. Don't count your money. (That pile of cash or chips in front of you; just don't count it.)
6. Don't let the last game affect your next game emotionally. (More on this below.)

These poker principles could be adopted, without modification, for use in trading, and this is exactly what I did. These rules served me well when I was an active short-term trader under market conditions that were conducive to short-term trading. In today's climate where longer-term position trading is the best strategy, most of these rules are still very relevant.

Take Principle 2; this is a rule I believe in to this day. There is absolutely no reason to discuss your position with anyone, especially while it is still open. It is another matter to want to discuss your trade with close confidants after you have closed out your position. Letting other people know what investments you currently hold, only makes it more difficult for you to admit that you are wrong should the investment go sour. Why? Because human nature is such that no one likes to admit to other people that they have been wrong. Now if it were only you who knew about the investment, it would still be hard to admit you're wrong, but not quite as painful. One frequent consequence of making your investments public is that you will tend to hang on to a losing position much longer than you would otherwise.

Principle 3 simply reiterates what every good trader or investor knows: Patience—waiting for the best trades only is critical. You need to be very selective, and you must not hesitate when it comes to taking your losses.

Principle 4 relates to position sizing. This can be a complex subject and there are many factors to be taken into account before you decide how big a position you should put on. The bottom line is that you must learn to vary your position size depending on how confident you are—based on your own trading principles. Increasing position size, or adding to your position is an integral part of being a consistently profitable trader. More on this in Rule 23 below.

In trading, Principle 5 says that you should not think about your account balance. Constantly thinking about how your account is doing can influence your trading in negative ways. Some traders like to set themselves daily, weekly or monthly targets. If that works for you fine. But be aware that the desire to meet your target can cause you to gamble on high-risk trades that you would normally reject. And in a good month where you have met your target early, there will be the tendency to ease back and not take perfectly good trades.

Finally, Principle 6: Every trade is separate from all previous trades. For traders, if you can slay this demon, you are virtually assured of profits. I will discuss the problem of Revenge Trading associated with losing trades in the section on "Rules Most Traders Won't Be Able to Follow". However at this point, I should mention that big winners can also impact your subsequent trading. Some traders tend to ease up, become less combative, after closing a big winner (as when they meet their target early) while others become over confident feeling that they now have a "profit cushion" and become less focused. By right, you want to just stick to your strategy and take any opportunity the market offers.

3. Always Have a Plan

Impulsive trading is a huge enemy of the individual investor-trader. You will fall victim to impulsive entries and exits throughout your early years in the markets. Impulsive trades are virtually guaranteed losers. Should you win from an impulsive trade, then you are in even bigger trouble because you are only reinforcing a bad habit that will lose you a whole lot of money over the long term.

You won't be able to eliminate it altogether, but a sure way to control impulsiveness in the markets is to have a trading plan. Not just a mental plan, but one that is written out, printed and preferably in your pocket all the time you are in the markets. OK, so today you might have your plan on your smart phone or tablet. But the idea is that it must be constantly accessible and you should be reading it every chance you get. Reading the plan repeatedly will reinforce it and keep at bay the "demons" that will try and suck you into trades you want no part of.

There is one caveat though. Sometimes developing a trading or investment plan can lead to "analysis paralysis". In trading, the problem is not so much a case of over-analyzing the possible scenarios, but more a case of getting overwhelmed by the potential risks. There will always be risks in any trade obviously. As long as the risks are within your limits of tolerance and your trade includes proper risk management (like a stop loss point, for example), you cannot let potential risks stop you from considering a trade.

4. Don't Fight the Primary Trend

This is an extremely powerful and important rule and one that I firmly believe in. Strangely, it has been my experience that many people new to the markets are less convinced by this rule than they should be. I believe the reason might be because many new traders are out hunting for tops and bottoms. They want to go for the kill, catch the turning points where the most money is to be made—if you get it right! Attempting to pick tops and bottoms, especially when you are new to the game can be treacherous; it is usually a mistake. Sure, billionaire hedge fund manager Paul Tudor Jones may pick tops and bottoms (See "Market Wizards",[71] "Paul Tudor Jones-The Art of Aggressive Trading"). But the underlying philosophy here is, don't break the rules until you have mastered them. Mere mortals like you and I, will almost never get to the point where we should be fighting the primary trend. So, just stick with the rule; stick with the major trend.

There is often a tendency to want to go counter-trend, that is, take a position against the prevailing trend. Say you are an investor who likes a particular sector, and you see a stock in that sector that is in a multi-month decline. You also see another stock in the same sector that is showing an uptrend. The rule is clear, stick with the trend until it bends, then hop off and take your profits. So, as an investor you should buy the stock trending up. But you'll be surprised how many individual investors will buy the declining stock, ostensibly because it is "cheap".

Not following the trend will hurt you, but there is one situation in which it can sting you particularly badly. That is when you are firmly committed to a trend but still end up *losing* money. To be committed to a trend and not make any money is not unusual; if you don't take a position you won't make any money even if you are sure the market is going up or down. But I know of many cases where a trader firmly believes in the overall trend of a market, but still loses money because he *messed with the counter-trend moves*. Believe me, this kind of loss can leave you in despair, killing your confidence and your motivation in addition to making you poorer.

There are many reasons why someone who firmly believes in the prevailing trend will still execute a counter-trend trade. Sometimes the sheer pain of a missed opportunity can make a trader do an impulsive trade in the hope that if it's a winner, the pain of the missed opportunity will be alleviated. Typically this type of trade will be in the direction opposite to the missed opportunity, that is, counter the prevailing trend. The trade makes you feel good temporarily but usually is a loser. If ever you need to compensate for a missed trade, only enter in the same direction as the missed trade, preferably on a pullback. Your entry will likely be at a price worse than you had originally targeted, but provided market conditions still support the trade, you stand more of a chance of making a profit than if you trade counter-trend.

A related rule is, "Don't try to dance between the raindrops". That is, don't try to catch every little wiggle in the market, every counter-trend move. This is an affliction suffered particularly by the active short-term trader who just needs action all the time. Never let boredom influence your trading; it can empty your pockets really fast. Again, stay with the bigger trend and ignore the retracements.

The longer-term investor can also be seriously affected by this tendency to "dance between the raindrops". In this case, the investor decides to get out of her position because she sees a correction taking hold. The plan is to buy back in at a lower price. However, once she has liquidated her position, the market turns around and, unwilling to buy back in at a higher price, the "long-term" investor is now left without a position. The rule here is: Never lose your position in a bull market. You must develop a fear of losing your position.

Having said all the above, you need to be alerted to some of the nuances of the rule "Don't fight the trend". Most significantly, the time frame of the trend must match your investment time frame. If you intend to hold an investment for a couple of years, the trend you see on an hourly chart will have little significance obviously. You should look instead at trends on a weekly or monthly chart. Another point to note would be the nature of the market you are trading. Some markets display clearer trends than others. If a market has a history of being particularly choppy, this rule will have little meaning.

5. Losers Average Losers
There is a photo of hedge fund manager Paul Tudor Jones in which, pinned to the wall behind him, you can clearly see this rule written out. There are many ways of stating this rule with perhaps the more usual being: "Don't average down". The old saying is that "professionals average up, while amateurs average down".

6. You Should Feel Good *After* Entering a Position
In trading, what is important is how you feel *after* you have done something. Many novice traders and investors feel very excited about entering a position, especially if it is based on some "information" they have been given by a "very reliable" source. So they feel good before they pull the trigger and even while they are accumulating their position. However, once they are fully in

and fully committed, the earlier excitement and exhilaration quickly turns into fear. These are the signs of an impulsive or insufficiently researched trade or investment. If the investment was well researched and carefully considered, based on sound criteria and a definite plan, then you should feel very comfortable *after* entry. Retracements, even big ones, will not shake you.

What Works in Trading, Often Works in Life in General

There are many rules that work in trading, and work in life as well. There are many parallels between trading and life in general. Trading and sport, for instance have much in common. Trading success, like success in any worthwhile human endeavor, requires years of training, experience, discipline, a love for what you do, etc. It is no surprise that the best trading coaches are also coaches of top-notch sportsmen and women.

7. Focus on the Target and Stop Checking Prices

I have an analogy between driving and trading; yes driving your car. It goes like this: If you are late to work, do you keep checking the time as you drive? Well you shouldn't because it only distracts you from focusing on your driving, makes you more anxious and more prone to making a mistake. You should forget about the time and focus only on your goal of getting to work as quickly and as safely as possible.

The analogy with trading or investing is quite obvious; when you are in a trade, focus only on the process, do not continually check prices or look at short-term charts. If you keep checking prices, you are very likely to put yourself in danger of ditching your plan and acting on an impulse, that is, of making a mistake. Once in a position, focus on your goal, your targets.

8. Prices Are Where They Are for a Reason

When you are faced with two lanes in a queue, are you the type who takes the longer or the shorter lane? Well we all know the longer lane is longer for a reason, and more often than not, it ends up being the faster lane. But it is sometimes difficult to resist the shorter lane. The analogy between this everyday event and trading can be seen in many different situations. The basic premise is that prices are where they are for a reason. That reason might not be obvious to us from where we stand, but very often, doing the less obvious, like taking the longer route, will prove to be the more profitable.

9. You Must Feel Uncomfortable

If it feels good, comfortable or easy, it's probably the wrong thing to do. Have you noticed how it often feels so good when you are "chasing a market"? (For example when buying into a rapidly rising market.) Well feeling good is *bad*. The markets are counterintuitive, hence the correct course of action will typically feel difficult to implement. It's when you're finding it really hard to pull the trigger that you should be doing it. The best traders take on trades that no one else is willing to.

10. When You Find Yourself Asking for Advice, You Know You're in Trouble

Asking for advice is a sure sign that you are losing faith in your original plan. And if you find yourself asking your *broker* for advice, it is in my opinion as sure a sign of trouble as you can get. When this happens, you should just get out.

11. Don't Be Part of the Herd Except...

The crowd is always wrong at the beginning and the end of a trend, but is correct through the middle of a trend. So, in the middle phase of a raging bull or bear market, do not go contrarian—the crowd/herd/consensus will be right and you will get trampled. There are many contrarians who have been wiped out by the stampeding herd; hedge fund manager Victor Niederhoffer being a famous example.

At the extreme of a trend, bull or bear, the consensus view is very strongly on one side. That is, everyone is agreed and there are no more traders to take new positions in the direction of the trend. On a grand scale, this is what happens as bubbles are about to burst. As an investor, when consensus reaches extreme levels, you should be tightening your stops and certainly not adding to your positions anymore.

Sir John Templeton classified the various phases of a bull market as follows: "Bull markets are born on pessimism, grow on skepticism, mature on optimism, and die on euphoria." Going with this classification, the crowd will be wrong during the early pessimism and late euphoria phases.

12. If You're Not 100 Percent OK, Take a Trading Break

So you had an argument with your spouse this morning, or your dog is seriously ill and you're upset, or you yourself feel like you're coming down with the flu; there is only one course of action, *don't trade*. Don't make any investment decisions.

The trouble with trading is that we tend to get obsessive about it. It is often so difficult to shut down the terminals and just go home, or go sit on a park bench somewhere and meditate or something. Whenever I think of this rule I am reminded of Martin Schwartz's great book, "Pit Bull: Lessons from Wall

Street's Champion Trader"[76]. He writes a lot about the perils of becoming addicted to trading, an affliction he admits to have suffered from. If you can't stop trading when *you want to*, you have a problem. Addiction to trading is especially an issue for short-term traders, particularly the very short-term traders or scalpers. Marty Schwartz was a scalper.

Many of the most famous traders advocated taking breaks: Jesse Livermore, Richard Dennis, Ed Seykota and even Marty Schwartz, all took frequent trading breaks.

Over the first few days of not trading you may suffer some withdrawal symptoms but eventually the urge to trade will wear off. After your break you will come back psyched up. One added benefit of taking a break is that it helps you to see the bigger market trend a lot more clearly.

When you're trying to take money out of someone else's pocket, you have to be at your extreme best, physically, mentally and emotionally. Drive, zeal, being in the zone, are all very important. Without them you can't win.

13. Never Let Your Expectations Make You Break Your Rules

When experienced traders talk about books dealing with the psychology of trading, one of the favorites will invariably be, "Trading in the Zone" by Mark Douglas[77]. The rule discussed here is courtesy of Douglas. He puts it like this, "We have to be rigid in our rules and flexible in our expectations." And he adds, "At this point, it probably goes without saying that the typical trader does just the opposite: He is flexible in his rules and rigid in his expectations."

This is powerful advice. Let me give you an example of a situation where this rule would apply: It's 2011 and you expect the price of silver to hit US50 dollars a troy ounce because that was the old historic high and you felt it was a powerful magnet. You have etched this price target into, not only your trading plan, but also your psychology. This is your expectation and it has become rigid. At the same time you have a rule that says you will use a trailing stop of US$5, that is, should the price drop US$5 from the high, you will liquidate your position.

As fate would have it, silver rallies to a high of about US$48, just shy of your US$50 target, on April 29, 2011 before plunging 20 percent in four days. It slices through your trailing stop which should be at about US$43, but you do nothing. Why? Because your expectation (US$50 target) is rigid while your rule (US$5 trailing stop) has become flexible. The price bounces around for a while and you still rigidly hold on to your expectation, and your rules are all but abandoned. Eventually, as the price corrects further, you throw in the towel and exit your position below US$30. This is a typical scenario which many a trader has lived through. What you need to etch into your psychology is not your expectation but the rule: Keep expectations flexible, rules rigid.

14. Mental Rehearsal Is Important

Mentally work through all alternative scenarios. Go through the motions of entering your trade, getting stopped out or taking profit, as documented in your trading plan. Do this continually until you are out of the trade. Mental rehearsal will make it easier for you to execute your plan.

However there is one caveat. Do not mentally rehearse the *amount of money* you are going to make should your target be hit.

Just focus on the number that represents your target. This number could be a stock price, an Index level, etc. You must make a deliberate effort to block out thoughts about the money you stand to make from a trade and focus instead on the exit level. Why? Thinking about the money will only make your expectation more rigid which is a problem as I elaborate in Rule 13. So, do not think in terms of the money, *or worse still what you can buy with that money.* Mentally rehearse only the entry and exit points and play the game according to your plan.

15. Widely Anticipated Bad News, When It Comes out, Will Send Markets Up

This is one of my favorites and it is especially effective in the stock market where there is a more even mix of professional and non-professional participants. The reverse of the above is also true of course, "Widely anticipated good news, when it comes out, will send markets down." No rule will make you money 100 percent of the time. But this rule is powerful. Watch out for opportunities to exploit it.

There are numerous examples throughout history that validate this rule. One of the more dramatic was the situation leading up to the first Iraq war. From the day Iraq invaded Kuwait on August 2, 1990 to the start of the U.S.-led air campaign on January 16, 1991, the stock markets of the world were in a funk. The news was bad, a war with Iraq was imminent, unavoidable. Yet on the very day the missiles started raining down on Baghdad, stock markets started a steep ascent, quickly recovering all of the recent losses. You don't need a war to invoke this rule. Much less dramatic events can have the very same effect. For example, a company result that is widely anticipated to come in very weak and actually does, will more likely send the company's share price up. Similarly, a widely anticipated strong economic number, when it comes out, will typically send the markets down.

For a recent illustration of this rule we need only go back to December 18, 2013. On that day, the U.S. Federal Reserve announced the first cut in its bond buying program. This much anticipated, and dreaded start of "tapering" (tapering of quantitative easing) sent the stock market soaring to record highs. The Dow Jones Industrial Average jumped 292 points or 1.84 percent to 16,167 while the S&P 500 index gained 30 points (1.67 percent).

The key to this rule is that the news must be *widely anticipated*. But what if the news is not widely anticipated? We can gain some insight into the strength of the prevailing trend by noting the market's reaction to *unanticipated* bullish and bearish news. A market that does not fall on bearish news is a strong market. Similarly, a market that does not rally on bullish news is signaling weakness.

16. The Snake That's Going to Bite You Is Not the One You're Watching

The issue that everyone is focused on will usually not be the one to trip up the market. Instead it will be something out of the blue, something the masses are blissfully unaware of. (I think I like this rule mostly because of the way it's worded.)

17. Boring, Sideways Markets Will Empty Your Pockets

Traders and investors must learn to sit out markets that are range-bound. These are difficult markets because you are constantly enticed into thinking a breakout is about to occur. Some of your trading signals will flash prematurely. Setups will look like the real thing only to fail quickly and catch you in a whipsaw. Again, avoiding sideways markets, is easier to do for the major-trend seeking investor than for the adrenalin-charged short-term trader. Don't worry about missing the big move. When volatility comes, it takes time to dissipate offering you many opportunities. Good entries and exits are typically made during periods of fear or frenzy, not boring sideways action.

Boredom, the need for activity, is never a good reason to enter a trade or investment. If you are a full-time trader, you may be doing trades because you feel like you should be working all the time. Forcing a trade when none is available that meets your criteria, will almost invariably lead to a loss. When you try to force a trade out of the market, you tend to see what you want to see, rather than what is really there. You will block out information that makes the trade uncertain and only see the positives. The idea is to stay objective and take only what the market offers, when it offers it. If you have been impulsive and have entered an investment that does not meet your criteria, there is only one option; get out immediately. To be fully engaged with the market and yet do nothing, is not easy. It is this kind of self-mastery that separates the successful trader-investor from the rest.

18. If You Have to Win, You Will Lose

For traders and investors the saying "money makes money" has even more meaning. If your room rent and your grocery bill are going to get paid from your trading profits, you have no business being in the markets. You should instead be out looking for a regular job. Only trade with money you are prepared to lose because it will make a world of difference to your trading psychology. Always be sufficiently capitalized for the product and size you are trading. The well capitalized investor is invariably more patient, quicker to cut his losses, and more willing to ride winners. He is also comfortable staying out of the markets altogether. The trader who must win to survive will find it hard to do any of these things. As broker-turned-trader Brian Gelber says in "The Market Wizards"[71], "… when you don't care, you do well, and when you try too hard, you don't do well."

19. Never Make a Mistake…

… and do nothing about it. There's no avoiding them; even super traders make mistakes. Sometimes it's because of an impulsive action. Sometimes it's an error in reading our indicators, causing us to predict that the stock goes straight up from here, but instead it turns down after an initial rally.

While we cannot avoid mistakes, *we almost always recognize that we have made a mistake pretty soon after we have done it*; often almost immediately after. The secret is to develop the habit of addressing your mistake the minute you recognize it. You must learn to think and act without hesitation—seamlessly. An uncorrected mistake invariably leads to more and more mistakes. So the real rule is: If you recognize that you have made a mistake, don't hope, correct it immediately. As they say, the first cut is the cheapest.

20. Never Let a Profit Become a Loss

This rule does not mean that you should move your stop order to breakeven the second the price goes beyond your entry price. Give the trade some time to develop but with your stop firmly in place. Once you are in a comfortable position above your breakeven point, do not let the trade become a loser. In other words, based on your trading strategy, move your stop to breakeven as soon as you can, but no sooner.

21. Be a Lone Wolf

If you need convincing about the virtues of playing a solitary game, I recommend that you read, "How I made $2,000,000 In

The Stock Market"[78] by Nicolas Darvas. Darvas was a world famous ballroom dancer turned successful investor who did most of his trading in the 1950s. It's an interesting and educational read that stresses the benefits of working entirely alone. Working alone helps keep out the "noise" and lets you develop a system that will be repeatable. You just want to block out those rumors and tips anyway you can. The only views you finally act upon must be your own views. Only then will you have conviction in your trades.

By the way, the core of Darvas' strategy was really quite simple: You only buy in a bull market. Look for the leading sector or growth sector and then buy the leading stock in that sector. Many of the strategies outlined by William J. O'Neil in his CAN SLIM methodology[79], are similar to ideas expressed by Darvas.

22. Have a Positive Mental Attitude
Stating the obvious? Yes, but with a slightly different take. The following has been my personal experience in the markets. It may be different for you, but give it some consideration:

I find that very often the result you get from your trading will match your prevailing mood. For example, if you are feeling down and listless, basically feeling unenthusiastic and negative, don't expect your trading to lift your spirits. On the contrary, your trading results will tend to *endorse* your prevailing mood. Most dangerous of all is when you are feeling low but cannot pin down a reason for why you are feeling that way. Trading in this state will amount to *a search for a reason* to feel the way you do and hence will almost surely result in losses which then give you a reason for feeling lousy.

How do you benefit from this insight? Always work hard at feeling optimistic, feeling good with yourself, feeling happy and calm. Meditation or vigorous exercise can help. Always get a good night's sleep and a good rest over the weekend to recharge your batteries. When you are in an optimistic, happy state of mind, your trading results (basically winning) will endorse or match these positive feelings. Yes, always have a positive mental attitude; it will make you more money in the markets.

23. Get Position Size Right

Position sizing is an important issue. There are people who use complex models to determine the optimum position size for any particular trade. In this discussion I will address some of the issues you will have to consider with regard to position sizing.

What is important to realize from the outset is that you will need to increase your position size as you gain experience and confidence in the markets. It will be very difficult to make serious money if you remain a single lot trader all your life. Trading a bigger position also allows you greater flexibility because you will then be able to scale in and out of a position; which simply means that you don't have to get in or out of your position all at once. Instead, you can start with a smaller position and then add to that position on pullbacks (essentially average up) or when getting out, you can take profits on part of your position while riding the rest.

Another point I want to make about reducing position size when your investment is not working out is this: It is a good idea to reduce your position because you then reduce your risk, but maybe more importantly, the act of reducing your size has an important psychological effect on your mindset. The very act of reducing your position is an act of submission. You submit to the notion that your trade *may* be wrong. And this is an important psychological barrier to move past. It makes it easier for you to eventually cut your position entirely should that be warranted.

Increasing position size is a step you must take as your trading progresses, but remember to do it in baby steps. Also, only increase position size from a winning position. You never want to go bigger after a losing streak.

That initial move from one lot to two lots, or from 1000 shares to 2000 shares is typically the most difficult. You are after all increasing your size by 100 percent. Be ready and willing to get smaller again should you find the psychological burden too much to handle at the larger size. Persevere and you will eventually get there. As Ari Kiev points out in his book, "Trading in the Zone"[80] (same title as the book by Mark Douglas), "The biggest obstacle to great success is the reluctance to add when it is right. To be as successful as possible, traders must play bigger, but this action does not come without discomfort or risk." That is the price a trader-investor has to pay for an opportunity to grow and reach his goal.

24. Diversification Produces Average Results
Diversify, diversify, diversify, is a mantra you will hear often. And for good reason since a diversified portfolio ensures that you spread out your risk over many stocks (or asset classes). Note however that when you diversify broadly, you basically end up duplicating the market average. If that is your intension, then you might as well invest in an index-linked mutual fund or ETF (Exchange Traded Fund).

If you want to invest in individual stocks, then you should limit yourself to a few stocks, perhaps five or even just two or three.

This is the only way to beat the market averages and is what you should do when conducive market conditions present you with stocks that meet your investment criteria.

25. Use If-Not-Correct (INC) Stops

Whenever you enter a trade, you must already have a predetermined stop loss level at which you must get out. We shall refer to this stop as the "predetermined stop". Your predetermined stop may be based on a percentage loss or a dollar amount loss and it is always non-negotiable.

The rule I am recommending here goes like this: When you enter a trade or investment, you do so based on certain criteria. You do so because the investment meets certain conditions either technical or fundamental. If at any time, any of those important conditions are no longer valid, then you should exit the investment immediately *regardless of where your predetermined stop loss price may be.*

Let's consider an example: You decide that you want to buy and hold shares in a particular semiconductor company because electronic chip sales are forecasted to soar. According to this rule, you should continue holding those shares only for as long as the data confirms your reason for buying the shares. If at any time, industry data does not support your assumptions, you should get out immediately, *even though you have a predetermined stop loss level which is much lower.* In other words, you will be getting out at a much more favorable price should you employ If-Not-Correct (INC) stops then if you simply wait until your predetermined stop gets hit.

In the above example, I have focused on fundamental criteria, but note that the INC stop can just as effectively be used with a stop based on technical levels on the charts or a chart pattern.

Getting out on the INC stop will usually mean a small loss but can even show a profit. As soon as any of the criteria on which you based your entry is negated, you must get out. This is the basis of the INC stop.

While INC stops normally save you money, *you cannot do away with predetermined stops.* Every investment must have a non-negotiable stop loss level before entry. Sometimes, the INC stop never triggers, then you will have to resort to the predetermined stop to get you out.

Using an INC stop requires some effort since you have to be constantly monitoring your investment for any changes in the fundamental or technical conditions that were the reason for your investment. But this is no reason to get lazy and just rely on your last-resort, predetermined stops because INC stops will reduce your losses.

Lastly, while all stops require discipline to execute, INC stops are notoriously difficult to stick with and the reason is this: When your INC stop is triggered, you may only be losing a little (after all that is the whole point of an INC stop). While the investment criteria may have been invalidated, hence triggering the INC stop, the price is actually not very far from your entry price. You still feel pretty comfortable emotionally with the prevailing price and unrealized loss, causing you to ditch your INC stop and just hang on. Unfortunately, most individual investors only get out when they cannot bear the pain anymore, which is usually the worse point at which to exit. Learn to stick with your INC stops and you will be getting out while still comfortable and suffering only a small loss for your misadventure. More on sticking with your stops later.

26. Be Prepared to Leave Money on the Table

Mark Douglas in "Trading in the Zone" points out that for most traders, *leaving money on the table is more painful than taking a loss*. I have my own take on why we feel this way: By my thinking, a loss is the rightful outcome for being wrong, so it feels OK. But to be right and not take all your profits is just agony. The fear of losing is not as great as the fear of losing out. Needless to say, this is dangerous thinking.

Almost no investment, except an extremely lucky one, will see you getting out at the top of a move. Most of the time, you will be out before or after the top is in. And if you employ trailing stops—always a good idea—then you, by necessity, will leave some money on the table. Just don't beat yourself up over it. More importantly, check if you have stuck to your plan, and if you have, congratulate yourself and move on.

27. Learn to Cope with Losing Streaks

Every trader gets hit by a losing streak from time to time. Learning how to cope with them is really important. Firstly, what happens when you suffer a losing streak? After a losing streak you develop a fear of losing, quite understandably. As you lose confidence, you can experience what I call the "scared money syndrome". The scared money syndrome will result in "scared plans" where you either take profit too early or cut your losses too early without giving the investment a chance. Scared money never wins. Rely on your usual strategies to determine your entry and exit points and don't let nervousness affect your trading. Winning begets winning for a good reason; psychologically you are in a better place unlike after a losing streak when you are trading with scared money.

The only way I know of getting rid of a losing streak and the accompanying scared money syndrome is to **take an extended break**. Start trading again only after all the negative emotions have fully dissipated.

28. Enter as Others Capitulate

The best entries are made just as participants on the same side as your intended trade are giving up. Say you recognize a bullish trend in a stock and want to establish an initial position. The key is to wait for a pullback and then detect when many long traders are getting out of their long positions. Once you recognize this capitulation you should start accumulating your position. My own experience with this approach has been mixed. I am often able to detect the capitulation but only when I already have a position, that is, only when I have some skin in the game. It is for this reason that I developed the strategy of taking a small initial position in my intended investment to fully engage in the mood of the market; then piling in when I sense capitulation.

29. Keep Good Records

Good record keeping is important. There are many types of records that you can keep, but I believe the most important is the one where you document why you made a particular investment or trade. This account should include entry, exit and stop prices plus a print out or digital image of the annotated, relevant chart. It forces you to recap in detail the investment that you put on while it is still fresh in your mind allowing you to assess whether or not you have stuck with your original plan. Just as importantly, it gives you a chance to learn from the past; both the good moves you have made and the mistakes you should avoid. Mistakes have a habit of coming back to haunt you, even those that you're sure you have conquered.

If you are a long-term investor, as opposed to a rapid fire trader, the work involved in keeping good records will not be that taxing. Most individual investors just do the bare minimum. They keep a record of their entry, exit and net profit or loss. This level of record keeping is not sufficient. Alexander Elder, best-selling author of "Trading for a Living"[81] and "Come Into My Trading Room"[82] among other books, is a big advocate of keeping good records. If you want more information on this subject, I suggest you read his books.

By the way, I am not a big fan of constantly tracking your account balance, as I have discussed elsewhere. Invest according to plan, and your account will be just fine.

30. Use Chart Patterns

This is not a book about charting, which is a fascinating subject in itself. But I feel obliged to mention some patterns that investors can take advantage of, as an introduction to this subject. Before getting to the patterns themselves, I want to make two points on how to utilize chart patterns in our trading.

When using chart patterns, do not go hunting for them. That is, do not deliberately seek them out; rather, wait for them to just "pop out" at you. The problem with *hunting* for particular patterns is that you can end up acting *in anticipation* of them forming which can be very dangerous. Or, you may see patterns that aren't the real thing, essentially "forcing patterns" where none exist. To go hunting for a pattern against waiting for it to pop out at you, may be too subtle a distinction for some beginners to appreciate. But after working with chart patterns for some time, you will learn the difference.

The other point is that once you are committed to utilizing a particular pattern to interpret market action, learn to expect only the usual outcome, not the exceptional. For example, if a pattern is a consistent indicator of a move lower, then expect a move lower and act accordingly. Since no pattern is 100 percent reliable, this same pattern may sometimes result in an exceptional move, that is, a move higher. In certain situations your mind can play tricks on you and make you focus on the exceptional outcome rather than the usual. This typically happens when the usual outcome will require you to get out of your current position either with a loss, or before your target is reached. You must learn to fight this tendency. Now to some chart patterns.

Typically, just before a stock or any other instrument starts on a long-term uptrend after a long period of consolidation (or building a base) expect to see a final sharp dip or shakeout. I am not suggesting that you buy on this dip. Instead, wait for the uptrend to begin and be confirmed. So what use is detecting that final dip? It is important to note this pattern because it will increase your belief in, and your commitment to the new uptrend.

The reverse also happens when a market is about to break down. You often see an exhaustion-type surge before the down trend begins. If you aren't already out of your long position, you should seriously consider tightening your stops immediately.

One effect of these sharp spikes before major trends, it to *trap traders in or out* of the market. For example, an investor who is long a particular stock may get out of his position on the sharp sell-off, leaving him *trapped-out* of the market as it then rallies higher and develops into a major uptrend. Similarly, if you are into shorting stocks, you may initiate a short position as the stock spikes down, then leaving you *trapped-in* as the stock reverses and goes higher. Traders who are trapped-in like this, will end up fueling the uptrend as they buy to cover their short positions.

Another pattern that has served me well is the "lower double-top". This occurs when you see a chart forming a new high which is then followed by a double-top at a level below that high. This is usually a signal of more downside to come.

There are many other powerful chart patterns, like the cup and handle pattern, the head and shoulders pattern, Elliott Wave patterns, etc. Experiment with them in your trading and eventually settle on those that work best for you in *your* market at any one particular point in time. (Patterns sometimes work for months or years before becoming ineffective.)

Ensure that you are observing the pattern in the appropriate time frame. For example, if you are an investor, you will want to be looking out for patterns on the daily or weekly charts, not on a 5-minute chart. Also, restrict yourself to a few patterns that work for you. Having too many patterns (or setups) will result in you seeing trades everywhere, especially when you are emotional, for whatever reason, and are liable to over-trade.

The market is the ultimate insider. It always knows more than you do and it knows it earlier. Learn to read the market well and you will be privy to the best insider information. Reading charts and watching the tape (the quote screen) is how you read the market.

Breaking the Rules

Some popular rules just don't hold up to scrutiny and so should *not* be followed. In this chapter I will explain why I reject three widely held (though certainly not universal) beliefs. I do not

expect everyone to agree with my selection of rules that should
be broken.

1. If You Can Trade One Market, You Can Trade
Any Market

I don't agree. Many market gurus, especially those who trade
using charts only, will tell you that all instruments behave the
same way. Typically they will say that they can trade off a chart
without knowing what market or stock or commodity, etc. the
particular price chart represents. And yet, time and time again,
you will read that people who are successful in trading, almost
invariably *specialize* in one or two markets. Years of studying a
particular market, staring continuously at its charts, give these
successful traders an edge over the generalists.

Each market has its own idiosyncrasies. It has long been noted,
for instance, that commodity markets tend to show stronger
and smoother trends which also last longer than do equity instruments which typically suffer frequent and deep retracements.

The participants differ from one market to the next, requiring
different tactics. One market may be dominated by big institutions, like the S&P 500 Index futures contract, while others may
be dominated by individual investors and still others by algorithmic (computer driven) trading. Volumes traded on a daily
basis will vary widely from one market to the next. This is an
important factor for any trader to consider because it will
determine how big a position you can take comfortably or how
much you can scale up your trading size as you get more confident with the market.

Liquidity affects the behavior of a market, particularly during
periods of sudden, extreme stress. Less liquid markets tend to

be much more volatile (show more extreme moves up and down) than liquid markets. Depending on your temperament and trading strategies, you may or may not prefer higher volatility. In general, liquid markets tend to be more predictable in their behavior. Chart patterns are smoother. In the global market crash of 2008/09, all stock markets tumbled hard in reaction to the financial crisis. But smaller, illiquid, emerging markets plunged even more in relative terms.

There will always be the rare few who can multi-task and trade several markets at once. But to increase your odds of success, stick to one market. Get to know that market really well until you react to it almost intuitively. It could be the shares in a particular company, a particular currency pair or a particular commodity or stock index futures contract; what is important is to learn everything you can about that instrument. It does not matter whether you are a very short-term scalper or a longer-term investor; knowing what moves a particular market, knowing how it reacts to certain news events, etc. will increase your odds of trading profitably. And this will take time typically several years for short-term trading. One trader whose approach to short-term trading I like, and used to follow at one time, is Al Brooks. In his interesting book, "Reading Price Charts Bar by Bar"[68], Brooks describes his "minimalist" approach to trading with charts. Brooks has repeatedly said that it took him ten years before he became consistently profitable day trading essentially one product, the S&P 500 E-Mini futures contract. Anecdotal evidence points to his experience being the norm rather than the exception.

2. It's Where You Sell That Counts

You will hear many people say that it does not matter where you buy, it is where you sell that counts. I tend to disagree. I believe a good entry is everything.

Both entry and exit have an important bearing on your profit or loss obviously. But remember that during the *entire period that you spend managing your trade*, you only have your entry price to reflect on. If your entry is good, you feel confident, good about yourself, and can hold on for longer. If your trade fails, you lose less when stopped out and there should be many opportunities to get out at breakeven because of your superior entry. When you have a good entry, you don't compound your mistakes as with a bad entry. That is, because you feel good about your entry, because you feel you have done the right thing, you tend to continue to do the right thing as you manage your trade, including taking a quick loss if necessary.

3. It Never Hurts to Take Profits

This is something you will typically hear from your commission-based broker. Remember, many of the rules your broker favors are meant to profit him *not you*. Be wary of advice coming from your broker especially if that advice results in you doing more trades.

The truth is, it can hurt you to take profits—too soon. The twin cardinal rules of successful trading are cut your losses fast and let your profits run. If you don't let your profits run, you will never be able to cover the many more times you will have been forced to cut your losses. So resist the temptation to take profits too soon, even if you are being encouraged to do so. Learn instead to use a trailing stop, that is, move your stop loss level up first to breakeven and then to protect some of your unrealized profit. There will be some occasions when you would have been better off just taking a quick profit, because the market does a quick turn and stops you out at a worse price. But all you need are those few trades where the market just keeps going and going. In such trades, you will eventually be stopped out at a much more favorable level than where you were first tempted to take profit.

A widely acknowledged statistic is that 90 percent of all profits come from 3 to 10 percent of the trades or investments we make. This means that we just have to be patient, and when we are on a winner, we need to ride it for as long as possible. Accept the reality that the big winners will come only rarely.

One of the most famous quotes attributed to legendary trader Jesse Livermore from the highly acclaimed "Reminiscences of a Stock Operator" goes like this, "It never was my thinking that made the big money for me. It always was my sitting." And he goes on to say, "Men who can both be right and sit tight are uncommon. I found it one of the hardest things to learn. But it is only after a stock operator has firmly grasped this that he can make big money." (For this and other brilliant quotes from this 1923 investment classic visit the related Wikipedia page[83], or better still read the whole book online at the Project Gutenberg Consortia Center.)

It is difficult to fight the urge for immediate gratification and ride a winner, some believe even more difficult than cutting your losses short. The next time you are in a winning trade, take Jesse Livermore's advice and sit on your hands.

Rules Most Traders Won't Be Able to Follow

There is a saying out there: "A million will seek, a thousand will find, only one will follow." The secret to trading success is self-mastery. This section deals with those rules most traders find extremely difficult to follow precisely because self-mastery is, to put it mildly, so elusive.

You have always been proud of your self-discipline, and you are determined to do whatever it takes to succeed as a trader. But trust me, nine out of ten traders reading this will have great difficulty following all these rules. So what are these devilish rules that are going to get you?

Unfortunately the rules you will find most difficult to follow are also among the most important rules; these are rules that can make or break your trading career. It may be no coincidence that the statistics have repeatedly shown that 90 to 95 percent of traders fail. As I said at the start of this book, many of the things you will read here are typically not talked about much outside the financial services community. Clearly, knowledge is not the issue. Most traders have put in the hours to learn their trade and know what they should and should not do. But going with the saying at the start of this section; you have sought, you have found, now can you follow?

The Obvious Rules Are Also the Most Difficult to Follow

If you think about it, the things that are most difficult to do in life are typically those things that are so obviously good for us. And so it is with trading: Cut your losses, ride your winners, don't over-leverage and don't over-trade. These are deceptively simple rules, and at first you may be able to follow them, but sooner or later, you will be doing head butts against the wall over why you simply cannot follow these rules.

Instead of cutting their losers and letting their winners run, most retail investors routinely do the opposite, they cut their winners and let their losers run. (More on cutting your losses later.) I have already discussed riding your winners in a previous section.

Leverage and over-trading kill most individual traders. When you apply leverage in your trading or investing, you are basically limiting the number of times you can get it wrong. And since you will get it wrong often when you are learning to trade, leverage may knock you out of the game before you get going. So leverage is a big *no* during the early months or even years of your trading career.

Trading more often than you should, or over-trading, brings with it a whole host of problems, including the fact that it will slowly eat away at your account through brokerage costs. Short-term traders (scalpers, day traders, etc.) typically fall victim to over-trading. They feel the need to be grinding it out day after day. Investors, on the other hand, know that one good trade can bring in many months' or even a whole year's worth of winnings. Consequently, the investor is more patient, more willing to wait for only the best opportunities.

Revenge Trading

Over-trading can come in several forms, the most dangerous is probably **revenge trading**. In revenge trading you are driven to try and recoup your losses *immediately*. Again, the shorter the time frame you trade in, the bigger an issue revenge trading will be. You are at your most vulnerable immediately after closing out a trade with a big loss. At that moment, you are your own worst enemy; you become a super amateur trader again no matter how experienced you may actually be. So learn to walk away and don't trade for some time. And how long is some time? First and foremost, once you get kicked out of your trade, be strong, be prepared to go home without any position, just nursing your loss. If you are a position trader or investor, it could mean days or weeks before you initiate your next trade. The point is, all the emotion associated with the last big loss must have fully dissipated before you do another trade, which is why someone who trades a longer time frame, someone who does not have to get back in the market within a few minutes or hours, will have a better chance of not falling victim to revenge trading.

I Cannot Execute My Stops

Adhering to your stop loss points will be difficult for most investors and traders. How well you abide by your stops is an indication of your potential for successful trading. The inability to stick to your stop loss levels is a big negative. It is almost like wanting to drive without knowing how to use the brakes. Now is that disastrous or what!

Why do we fail to execute our stops? Why does our mind play tricks on us every time a stop loss level approaches, telling us to just ignore the stop, making us believe that this trade is a special case and should he handled differently? There are several reasons: One is the reluctance to turn an unrealized loss into a psychologically more painful realized loss and another is the fear that the market will immediately turn around as soon as you get out. Firstly remember that you can always reenter a position after you are stopped out, even if it means getting back in at a slightly worse price. Secondly, accept the fact that sometimes you will be wrong and you will be stopped out close to the turn, but that more often, sticking with your stops will save you lots of money.

One of my former clients has a favorite lament, "Why is it that I always have money to invest at market tops but never seem to have any money at market bottoms." If you have had this experience, take some comfort in the fact that you are not alone. Many individual investors get fully invested in bull markets and then get stuck with overvalued investments that they *refuse to take losses on.* The end result is that when the market corrects back to below the mean, these investors simply don't have the funds to invest. It is at this very phase that long-term institutional investors are scooping up stocks. The moral of this story is that you should always stay true to your stop loss levels because if you have stops for every investment and abide by them, you will never be entirely without investable funds.

There are several ways to improve adherence to your stop loss points. The first piece of advice you might hear is: Always use "hard" stops. Hard stops are stop loss orders that are entered into the trading platform, either by you or your broker. (In the old days hard stops were essentially stop orders you left with your broker who would then execute them as they were triggered.) By all means use hard stops especially if you are trading a liquid market where slippage will be less of a problem. (Slippage means the stops don't execute at the price you choose but at a worse price.) Hard stops are in most situations preferable to mental stops, that is, stops which you manually execute as price reaches the targeted level.

Slippage is not the main problem with hard stops though. The real problem is that, like a mental stop, there is little to stop you from canceling or moving them. So how can you be more disciplined when it comes to executing your stops?

Mental rehearsal can help. When setting a stop loss level, you must accept the amount of loss emotionally, only then can you trade calmly and execute the stop when required. Choose stop levels that are meaningful, perhaps chart-based, and become committed to them. You will find that a non-negotiable stop loss point that you have used for a long time, based on a fixed dollar loss (say $1000 per trade) or percentage loss (say a 10 percent loss), will be easier to stick with. This is because you have mentally rehearsed this stop over and over again, and you have become very committed to it. So always have a last resort, non-negotiable, predetermined stop. And last, but never the least, work hard on your If-Not-Correct-Stops, which are likely to be the most difficult to stick with.

Gunning the Stops

Choosing a proper stop loss point or level is more critical when trading short term. The danger here is that professionals frequently know where most of the stops will be and then "gun" those stops. That is, they move the market to trigger the stops. If you've heard yourself saying something like, "I always get stopped out right at the low (or high) of the move," then you are probably a victim of these raids on stop orders placed at obvious, widely watched support or resistance levels.

If you are a position trader or investor, then you will use wide stops which will be too far away for traders to try and trigger deliberately. This does not mean your stops can't be hit of course, only that they are less likely to be triggered by a gunning-the-stops operation.

Furthermore, in the current environment, where "mini flash crashes" (price spikes up or down that last seconds or less) can be quite common in certain markets, long-term investments with wide stops are less likely to be affected.

If your stops get gunned frequently, then you tend to lose faith in them and are more likely to ignore them or not use stop orders altogether.

I will end this section with another quote from the classic "Reminiscences of a Stock Operator", widely held to be a biography of one of Wall Street's greatest traders, Jesse Livermore: "Losing money is the least of my troubles. A loss never bothers me after I take it. I forget it overnight. But being wrong — not taking the loss — that is what does the damage to the pocket-book and to the soul." So if you find it difficult to cut your losses, remember that even the greatest traders have struggled with this issue.

So What Is Your "Anti-Edge"?

Most traders are familiar with the concept of having an "edge". An edge is basically any advantage that you may have over the rest of the traders you compete against in the markets. For some traders this edge takes the form of a superior trading system, perhaps based on some proprietary indicator. For others, their edge may simply be supreme self-discipline. I know a few traders whose edge is an enhanced skill at recognizing patterns in charts (pattern recognition). And of course we cannot leave out the Warren Buffets among investors who have the ability to pick out investments that represent great value based on their fundamentals. Please note that your edge cannot be "hard working" or "ambitious" or "persevering" or "strong willed". There are thousands of traders out there who have all these qualities in abundance; young traders with no job and little money who are willing to work eighteen hours a day, seven days a week. (Also, your edge *should not* be insider information or manipulative strategies which are both illegal of course.)

So that's an edge, but what is an "anti-edge". For sure, to be a successful trader, you need to have an edge. But successful trading is not only about having an edge; it is also about being competent in all other aspects of trading. My point is, if you have an edge, but then you are extremely weak in one other aspect of trading (e.g. patience, money management, focus, courage, etc.) then your edge will be negated by this Achilles' heel—your anti-edge. An edge is effective only if you are also strong in, or are managing in same way, *all* the different facets of good trading. Successful trading is difficult because, not only do you need to have an edge, you also *cannot afford to have an unresolved weak spot or anti-edge.*

An anti-edge is usually some kind of psychological issue that remains unresolved or unmanaged. It could be something like revenge trading, or the inability to increase size when appropriate. Recognize your anti-edge and do whatever it takes to conquer it. This usually means applying the appropriate trading rule with great discipline. To guarantee consistent profits, you must have an edge plus you must neutralize your anti-edge. Otherwise, at best, you will forever remain in breakeven limbo.

There Is No Holy Grail to Trading Success

Good and experienced traders are quite willing to share all their secrets with their mentees. Yes, despite the commonly held belief that the master always holds back his best ideas, profitable traders are really willing to share it all. Why? Because they know that while you may have their methodology, the vast majority of traders will not be able to implement the strategies *consistently*. And that is what profitable trading boils down to; not what you know or don't know, but what you know and can follow consistently. Remember, the profitable thing to do, the right thing to do, *is always the most difficult thing to do.*

Van Tharp, a leading authority on the psychology of trading makes the same point when he says that knowing a super trader's system is no guarantee of success, but being able to duplicate his psychology or mental state is.

The super traders are disciplined *all* the time. The rest of us will always have lapses in discipline. Keep the lapses in discipline to a minimum and you have a chance at navigating today's treacherous markets.

To be able to follow your own rules, you must be:

- In the right place psychologically
- Be sufficiently capitalized
- Have the right attitude towards money and profits
- Have the energy and mental stamina
- Understand that being disciplined means there are no exceptions

Understand why you behave the way you do when it comes to trading rules and work hard at overcoming your weaknesses.

Appendix A

"Flash Boys": The Book on HFT by Michael Lewis

Best-selling business writer Michael Lewis recently released his book on HFT titled "Flash Boys: A Wall Street Revolt"[69]. As always the Michael Lewis name and promotion machine together do the job of getting the book to number one on the best seller lists, and they manage to do it on the day of release. From Lewis' appearance on CBS' 60 Minutes, where he famously says that the "stock market is rigged" to numerous other interviews, Lewis creates quite a ruckus over the HFT issue. One particular "debate" on CNBC on April 1, probably better described as a brawl[70], will go down as one of the most infamous moments in business TV history.

It's a great story, and you should read it, but only to entertain yourself. If you want a critical look at HFT, or you want to learn more about the subject, this is not the book for it. Initially, I was concerned that I might have to rewrite parts of my book to accommodate new material coming out of Flash Boys. But that proved to be an unnecessary worry; there is very little that's new or adds to the HFT debate in Flash Boys.

The story of Brad Katsuyama and his launching of the IEX equity trading venue (a dark pool really) is an interesting one.

However, I feel that the approach taken by IEX represents an artificial dampener on innovation, and so intuitively, I can't see it becoming wildly successful. If it does, and this line on page 160, "They should seek to put all the other exchanges out of business" should by some miracle actually come about, then its déjà vu and we retail investors are in real trouble; don't expect to ever revisit penny-wide spreads again.

Michael Lewis accuses HFT of "front running" (in some places "electronic front running" or "legal front running"). This is way off the mark. Buying or selling when you sense or detect a big order is perfectly legitimate. It has been going on in markets for ages, even before the days when tape reading wonders like Jesse Livermore used to do it. This is not front running; you need clients to be front running and HFTs do not have clients. You can only front run an order, or instruction to trade; how can you front run a partial trade which is what Lewis is going on about.

There is one line on page 78 that's so ridiculous it's really quite funny. This nameless president of a $9 billion hedge fund decides to buy an ETF through his private online brokerage account. He says, "I hadn't done anything but put in a ticker symbol and a quantity to buy. And the market popped." Surely you jest Mr. President. If you believe this you'd believe the virus in your computer gave you the flu.

There are many other so called "issues" that are raised in Flash Boys, like colocation, the alleged huge profits being made by HFTs, the long periods that HFTs can go without a losing day, etc. These are issues that are either non-existent today or can be easily resolved if one took the time to do some serious research. Apparently Lewis set out with a thesis that would sell to a public that was already made receptive by the media onslaught against HFT; and then built a story around it. There was no intention to uncover the facts and analyze them critically; the conclusions were already set in stone from the outset, it would appear. Besides, how seriously should you take a book that is written with a movie in mind.

Finally, the one lasting impression I came away with after reading Flash Boys, is that it is more a book about badly behaving brokers and their uninformed institutional clients, than it is about the "ills" of HFT. Read the book, but don't be fooled: On balance, HFT is good for the longer-term retail investor. In fact she is the biggest winner.

Appendix **B**

In Publishing and Investing, the Little Guy Never Had It so Good

Or, parallels between what is happening in the financial markets and in publishing.

I like looking for analogous behavior, for parallels between industries. Examples of technological innovation disrupting industries are too numerous to list here. But in this commentary I'm more focused on how digital networks including the Internet of course, have transformed certain industries. The one that comes to mind most readily for the average person must be the travel industry. Travelling will never be like it was about two decades ago, with costs now way down while convenience and choice are way up.

As a self-publishing author I can't help but see the parallels between what is happening in the financial markets and in the publishing industry. I have been suggesting that the small guy of the securities industry, the retail investor, may actually be better off today because of the emergence of HFT. We certainly don't like how HFT can manipulate and disrupt markets, but we do like the way it is disrupting established hierarchies within the financial services industry. The entrenched establishment has for decades treated retail investors with disdain. Yet today, you actually see the little guy—disparagingly referred to as the "dumb money" for so long—being courted. Why? Because there is a new "big boy" in town: HFT. The establishment, the cozy interconnections among the preexisting established players is being rocked by the newcomers, by the KCGs, Citadels and Virtu Financials of this new era. The status quo is no more and the small guy is an indirect, collateral beneficiary.

The same kind of scenario is playing out in the publishing industry. New and unestablished writers (small players?) were always the step children of that industry. But no more. Enter Amazon's Kindle, Apple's iBooks, and Kobo, etc. to challenge the traditional publishers, the so called gatekeepers. The new players have turned the publishing industry on its head. And the beneficiary... the small gals and guys, the new or less established writer. It is fabulous to see this kind of empowerment taking place. Self-publishing writers everywhere are rejoicing. Traditional publishers throw everything they've got at the new-comers like Amazon's Kindle Direct Publishing, but things have changed and there is no going back to the way it used to be.

At the core of these changes is of course technology, specifically the growth and refinement we see in digital communications. Be it the Internet or super-fast digital networks connecting traders to exchanges, technology is reshaping our world and reshuffling the established hierarchy in many industries. And in the process, customers enjoy lower costs while businesses see their margins compressed. No tilted playing field is safe. The ultimate leveler, some innovative, network enabled application; an HFT-enabling electronic exchange, a self-publishing hub, or some-thing else, is out there and coming your way real soon.

Acknowledgements

To my old friend Steve Khoo, I owe a great debt. He has constantly encouraged me throughout this project and kindly read through the manuscript making valuable suggestions that I have incorporated into the final version. Big thanks are also due to Rashid Bax and Charles for their support and help, especially in reviewing the final draft.

References

[1] Edward Allen Toppel. "Zen in the Markets". Warner Books (1992)

[2] Jon Najarian and David Russell. "Leap Wireless Calls Spike Ahead of Deal". The Street (July 15, 2013)

[3] Katya Wachtel. "AUDIO: Listen To Raj And Danielle Chiesi Revel In Their Trading Of Akamai Stock Ahead Of A Public Guidance Announcement". Business Insider (April 5, 2011)

[4] Wiretap of call between Goldman Sachs director Rajat Gupta and Galleon Group founder Raj Rajaratnam. Wikimedia Commons (July 29, 2008)

[5] Press Releases: "Manhattan U.S. Attorney And FBI Assistant Director-In-Charge Announce Insider Trading Charges Against Four SAC Capital Management Companies And SAC Portfolio Manager". United States Attorney's Office Southern District of New York (July 25, 2013)

[6] F.B.I. Statement on SAC's Guilty Plea. (November 5, 2013)

[7] "To Catch a Trader". Frontline/PBS Documentary Transcript (January 7, 2014)

[8] "To Catch a Trader". Frontline/PBS Documentary (January 7, 2014)

[9] Dylan Mathews. "Insider trading enriches and informs us, and could prevent scandals. Legalize it". The Washington Post Wonkblog (July 26, 2013)

[10] James Harris Simons. "Mathematics, Common Sense, and Good Luck: My Life and Careers". Speech at MIT (December 9, 2010)

[11] Chris Larson. "Quant Funds Feel Investor Bite After Underperforming". Bloomberg.com (February 19, 2014)

[12] Eric Onstad. "Lasers, microwave deployed in high-speed trading arms race". Reuters (May 1, 2013)

[13] Manoj Narang. "A Much-Needed HFT Primer for 'Flash Boys' Author Michael Lewis". Institutional Investor (April 7, 2014)

[14] Christopher Faille. "Really Fast Information Processors or Tippees?" AllAboutAlpha.com (January 27, 2014)

[15] Bianca Hartge-Hazelman. "High-frequency trading is 'legalised scalping'" The Sydney Morning Herald (April 10, 2014)

[16] SGX Singapore Exchange website

[17] Irene Aldridge. "High-Frequency Trading: A practical guide to Algorithmic Strategies and Trading Systems" Second Edition. John Wiley and Sons, Inc. (2013)

[18] Scott Patterson. "Dark Pools: The Rise of the Machine Traders and the Rigging of the U.S. Stock Market". Crown Business (June 2012)

[19] Tyler Durden. "HFT Pays: CEO Of Firm That Accounts For 5% Of US Equity Volume Selling His NY Mansion For $114 Million" Zero Hedge (December 23, 2013)

[20] Larry Tabb. "The End Of High Frequency Trading As We Know It?" TABB Forum (October 1, 2012)

[21] Zachary Warmbrodt. "Automated traders woo farm groups". POLITICO (February 2014)

[22] Bruno J. Navarro. "Vanguard CIO: High-Frequency Trading Cuts Costs". CNBC (October 18, 2012)

[23] EPTA. "What others Say About HFT". FIA-EPTA Blog

[24] Karen Freifeld. "UPDATE 2-New York's Schneiderman seeks curbs on high-frequency traders" Reuters.com (March 18, 2014)

[25] Kris Devasabai. "Quants turn to AI for market insights" Hedge Funds Review (December 20, 2013)

[26] "Concept Release on Equity Market Structure". SEC (January 2010)

[27] Sal L. Arnuk, Joseph C. Saluzzi. "Broken Markets: How High Frequency Trading and Predatory Practices on Wall Street are Destroying Investor Confidence and Your Portfolio". FT Press (June 2012)

[28] Andrei A. Kirilenko, and Andrew W. Lo. "Moore's Law vs. Murphy's Law: Algorithmic Trading and Its Discontents". (March 19, 2013).

[29] "CFTC Orders Panther Energy Trading LLC and its Principal Michael J. Coscia to Pay $2.8 Million and Bans Them from

Trading for One Year, for Spoofing in Numerous Commodity Futures Contracts". CFTC (July 22, 2013)

[30] "FINDINGS REGARDING THE MARKET EVENTS OF MAY 6, 2010: REPORT OF THE STAFFS OF THE CFTC AND SEC TO THE JOINT ADVISORY COMMITTEE ON EMERGING REGULATORY ISSUES" (September 30, 2010)

[31] James B. Stewart and Daniel Hertzberg. "Terrible Tuesday: How the Stock Market Almost Disintegrated A Day After the Crash". The Wall Street Journal (November 20, 1987)

[32] Andrei A. Kirilenko, and Albert S. Kyle, and Mehrdad Samadi, and Tugkan Tuzun. "The Flash Crash: The Impact of High Frequency Trading on an Electronic Market". (May 26, 2011)

[33] Scott Patterson. "Did Shutdowns Make Plunge Worse?" The Wall Street Journal (May 7, 2010)

[34] Julie Creswell. "Speedy New Traders Make Waves Far From Wall St." The New York Times (May 16, 2010)

[35] Scott Patterson. "How the 'Flash Crash' Echoed Black Monday". The Wall Street Journal (May 17, 2010)

[36] VPRO Backlight Documentary. "Money & Speed: Inside the Black Box (Marije Meerman)" VPRO Backlight (December 13, 2012)

[37] Kara M. Stein, Commissioner. "Remarks before Trader Forum 2014 Equity Trading Summit". U.S. Securities and Exchange Commission (February 6, 2014)

[38] Summary of Haim Bodek Presentation. "HFT (Scalping)-An Artificial Industry Explained". Themis Trading Blog (June 18, 2013)

[39] Danielle Kucera and Douglas MacMillan. "Facebook Investor Spending Month's Salary Exposes Hype". Bloomberg (May 25, 2012)

[40] John McCrank. "Knight Capital posts $389.9 million loss on trading glitch". Reuters (October 17, 2012)

[41] Haim Bodek. "2013 TOP STORIES: HFT Checkmate – The Alpha in Order Types". TABB Forum (December 31, 2013)

[42] Haim Bodek. "The Problem of HFT - Collected Writings on High Frequency Trading & Stock Market Structure Reform". CreateSpace Independent Publishing Platform (January 2013)

[43] Jon Najarian. "High-Frequency Trading Is Making a Joke of the Markets". Yahoo Finance (July 12, 2013)

[44] Scott Patterson. "Firm Stops Giving High-Speed Traders Direct Access to Releases". The Wall Street Journal (February 20, 2014)

[45] VPRO Backlight Documentary. "The Wall Street Code (Marije Meerman)". VPRO Backlight (November 4, 2013)

[46] Alexandra Zendrian. "Vanguard's Gus Sauter Thanks High-Frequency Traders". Forbes (September 23, 2010)

[47] "The fast and the furious". The Economist (February 25, 2012)

[48] Peter Gomber, Björn Arndt, Marco Lutat, Tim Uhle. "High-Frequency Trading". Goethe Universitat (March 2011)

[49] Charles M. Jones. "What Do We Know About High-Frequency Trading?" Columbia Business School (March 2013)

[50] Jonathan Brogaard, Terrence Hendershott and Ryan Riordan. "High Frequency Trading and Price Discovery" ECB Working Paper Series (November 2013)

[51] Dave Lauer. "2013 TOP STORIES: HFT – In Search of the Truth". TABB Forum (December 27, 2013)

[52] Bernard S. Donefer. "High-Speed Trading Is Progress, Not Piracy". Bloomberg View (April 10, 2012)

[53] Joseph Saluzzi and Sal L. Arnuk. "HFT Pirates and Their Academic Friends" The Big Picture (April 16 & 18, 2012)

[54] John A. McCarthy, Christopher R. Concannon, Leonard J. Amoruso. "Proposal to Increase the Obligations of NMS Market Makers" (July 9, 2010)

[55] "RECOMMENDATIONS REGARDING REGULATORY RESPONSES TO THE MARKET EVENTS OF MAY 6, 2010" Joint CFTC-SEC Advisory Committee

[56] Stanislav Dolgopolov. "High-Frequency Trading, Order Types, and the Evolution of the Securities Market Structure: One Whistleblower's Consequences for Securities Regulation" (January 23, 2014)

[57] Gary Cohn. "The Responsible Way to Rein in Super-Fast Trading". The Wall Street Journal (March 20, 2014)

[58] Colin Clark. "Updating the Market-Wide Circuit Breaker". NYSE Euronext (October 10, 2011)

[59] NASDAQ OMX. "Frequently Asked Questions Market-Wide Circuit Breakers".

[60] BATS. "BATS Limit Up/Limit Down FAQ" (January 31, 2014)

[61] NYSE EURONEXT. "Limit Up/Limit Down Overview and Updated Testing Schedule". (January 7, 2013)

[62] Matthew Philips. "How the Robots Lost: High-Frequency Trading's Rise and Fall". Bloomberg Businessweek (June 6, 2013)

[63] Michael P. Regan and Sam Mamudi. "Son of Big Board Father Is No Friend to NYSE". Bloomberg.com (Feb 5, 2014)

[64] Emily Flitter. "Former stock market 'scalpers' are vocal HFT critics". Reuters.com (October 3, 2012)

[65] Molly McCluskey. "The Real Story About Investors and Trading Fiascoes". The Motley Fool (September 14, 2012)

[66] "Trading firm Virtu Financial plans to raise up to $100 million in IPO". Reuters (March 10, 2014)

[67] Michelle Celarier. "NY attorney general targets high-frequency trading". New York Post (March 18, 2014)

[68] Al Brooks. "Reading Price Charts Bar by Bar: The Technical Analysis of Price Action for the Serious Trader". Wiley (May 4, 2009)

[69] Michael Lewis. "Flash Boys: A Wall Street Revolt". W. W. Norton & Company (March 31, 2014)

[70] Steven Russolillo. "Highlights from the Brawl Over High-Frequency Trading". The Wall Street Journal MoneyBeat (April 1, 2014)

[71] Jack D. Schwager. "Market Wizards: Interviews with Top Traders". New York Institute of Finance (1989)

[72] Jack D. Schwager. "The New Market Wizards: Conversations with America's Top Traders". HarperCollins (1992)

[73] Edwin Lefevre. "Reminiscences of a Stock Operator". CreateSpace Independent Publishing Platform (2012) (First published 1923)

[74] Poker vs trading infographic. Tradimo.com (April, 2013)

[75] Poker Night on Wall Street. bloomberg.com (October, 2013)

[76] Martin Schwartz. "Pit Bull: Lessons from Wall Street's Champion Trader". HarperCollins (1998)

[77] Mark Douglas. "Trading in the Zone: Master the Market with Confidence, Discipline and a Winning Attitude". Prentice Hall Press (2001)

[78] Nicolas Darvas. "How I Made $2,000,000 in the Stock Market". Kensington Publishing Corp. (1986) (First published 1960)

[79] William J. O'Neil. "How to Make Money in Stocks: A Winning System in Good Times or Bad" Second Edition. McGraw-Hill, Inc. (1995)

[80] Ari Kiev. "Trading in the Zone: Maximizing Performance with Focus and Discipline". John Wiley & Sons, Inc. (2001)

[81] Alexander Elder. "Trading for a Living: Psychology, Trading Tactics, Money Management". Wiley (1993)

[82] Alexander Elder. "Come Into My Trading Room: A Complete Guide to Trading". Wiley (2002)

[83] Reminiscences of a Stock Operator. Wikipedia.org

About the Author

Combining a passion for the markets with forty years of experience, veteran global investor and trader Chandra Kumar is always thinking about how the markets impact individual investors and traders. For the past twenty years he has worked full-time in the markets, as a broker, trader and a Local scalping in the futures markets. He now describes himself as a professional scalper displaced by the machines, and spends his time looking out for good longer-term position trades. He is still trying to figure out how his Ph.D. in Geology is going to help him in the markets.

You can contact the author via the following:

Email: gabbrobooks@gmail.com

Twitter: @gabbrobooks

www.gabbrobooks.com

Index

A

Abenomics, 5, 7
Accenture, 34
account balance, tracking, 90
advice, seeking, 96
affirmative obligation, 50
Aldridge, Irene, 22
algorithmic trading, 39
    defined, 15, 16
amateurs against professionals, 76
analysis paralysis, 91
anticipated news, 100
anti-edge, 123–124
Apple, 34
arbitrage, 27, 48–49, 56
    ETF, 28
    feedback loop, 39
    multiple exchanges, 28
    S&P 500 futures, 27
    SPY, 27
artificial intelligence, 17
automated trading. *See* algorithmic
    trading

B

bacteria, HFT like, 73
bad HFT neutralizing, 59
balanced arguments, 23
ballroom dancer, 104
Bank of Japan. *See* BOJ
BATS Exchange IPO, 42
Bharara, Preet, 11
Black Monday, 35–36, 38–40
Bodek, Haim, 42–45, 65

BOJ, 5–6
breaks, trading, 98, 110
brilliant graduates, 17
broker, 116
Brooks, Al, 79, 115
Buffet, Warren, 28, 47
bull market, 82, 84
buy-and-hold, 7–8, 77

C

CAN SLIM, 104
cancelation, orders, 31
capitalized, sufficiently, 102
capitulation, 110
central banks, 5, 7
chart patterns, 111
checking prices, avoid, 95
circuit breakers, 36, 40, 61
    likely to work, 63
Cohen, Steve A., 11
colocation, 20–21, 30, 52–53
    complexity of the market
        structure, 53
    worldwide, 21
commodity futures, 32
communications technology, 19
confidence, individual investors, 70
counter-trend, 92, 93
Cramer, Jim, 3
currency devaluation, 7
currency wars, 7
cut losers, 119

D

d'Estaing, V. G., 8

dark pools, 54
Darvas, Nicolas, 104
dealers, 26
decision-making algorithms, 16
decline, HFT, 64
deer in the headlights, 87
derivatives, 8
designated market maker, 26
direct data feeds, 30, 48
directional strategies, 28
discretionary trader, 86
discussing open positions, 89
disruptive HFT, 33
diversified portfolio, 106
documentary
    Money & Speed, 40
    The Wall Street Code, 48
    To Catch a Trader, 12
Dollar, U.S., 8
Donefer, 49
Douglas, Mark, 98, 109
dumb money, 132

E

ECB, 5
edge, 123
electronic trading, 26
entry versus exit, 116
execution algorithms, 16
exercise, 105
Exorbitant Privilege, The, 8
expectations, 98

F

F.B.I., 11
Faber, Marc, 7
Facebook IPO, 42
Federal Reserve, 5
feedback loop, 39
fiber-optic cables. *See* optical fiber
    cables

Flash Boys, 127
Flash Crash, 33–34, 37–41, 60
    canceled orders, 35
    documentary, 40
    prevent, 61
    trigger, 37
flash order, 46
front running, 47, 128
funds, 1, 66
    mutual, 1
    pension, 1
    sovereign wealth, 1, 78
futures markets, 23, 54, 57

G

global financial crisis, 3, 4, 7, 71
Gold Reserve Act, 4
Goldman Sachs, 31, 60
good and bad HFT, 23
good HFT, 48
Great Depression, 7
Greenspan, Alan, 5
gunning stops, 42, 122

H

halt, trading, 56
hard stops, 121
Hash Crash, 29
hedge funds, insider trading, 10
HFT, 18
HFT Scalper model, 55, 56
HFT Scalping, 55
HFTs, 18
high frequency trading
    characteristics, 18
    decline of, 64
    feuding, 22
    good and bad, 23
    positives, 74
    profit every day, 71
    very short-term, 19

volumes globally, 20
what is, 18
winners and losers, 65
winning percentage, 19
holding period, stocks, 77

I

IEX, 127
If-Not-Correct stops, 107
impulsive trading, 91
INC stops, 107
individual investors, 1, 6, 24, 60, 73
    confidence, 70
    participation, 2–4
    speed disadvantage, 70
    strategies, 83
    winners, 68
INET conference, 8
informational advantage, 53
insider trading, 47
    defined, 8
    government crackdown, 10
    hedge funds, 10
    LEAP Wireless, 9
    legal, 9
    legalize, 13
    U.K. regulator, 12
    U.K.'s biggest case, 12
institutional investors, 66
intermediation, 25
intuitive, 86
investors, bothered by machine
    trading, 71

J

Japan, 6

K

Katsuyama, Brad, 127
Kiev, Ari, 106
Knight Capital, 42

Knightmare, 42
Kudlow, Larry, 11

L

laser, 19
latency, 18–19
latency arbitrage, 30
layering, 30, 32
LEAP Wireless, 9, 10
legalize insider trading, 13
level playing field, 69
    less tilted, 70
leverage, 119
Lewis, Michael, 127
life and trading, parallels, 95
Limit Up-Limit Down, 41, 61
    likely to work, 63
liquidity, 26, 114
Livermore, Jesse, 117, 123
locals, 54
    defined, 2
long-term investing, 76–79
    advantages, 78
losing streak, 109
lower double-top, 113
LULD. *See* Limit Up-Limit Down

M

machine trading, 4, 71
machine-readable format, 47
maker-taker model, 27
manipulative HFT, 31–32
    neutralizing, 59
market making, 25, 48–50, 55, 56
    evolution, 57
    formal and informal, 26
    scandals, 26
Medallion Fund, 17
meditation, 105
mental rehearsal, 99
mental stops, 121

message traffic, 60
microwave, 19, 28
mini flash crashes, 40–42, 60
    algo glitches, 42
    gunning of stops, 42
    human error, 42
mistakes, 103
momentum ignition, 30
momentum strategies, 28
Money & Speed, 40

N

NASDAQ OMX, 19
negative obligation, 53
Nikkei 225, 6

O

O'Neil, William J., 104
online retail brokerages, 76
optical fiber cables, 19, 28
options market, 9
order anticipation, 29
over-trading, 119

P

Panther Energy Trading, 32
patience, 90
pioneering HFT, 54
plan, trading, 91
poker and trading, 88
poker player, 28
policy makers, 6
position sizing, 90, 105
predatory, 66
price spikes. See mini flash crashes
privileged HFT, 43, 52
privileges, 51–52
proposal from HFTs, 50
psychology, 87, 125
publishing industry, 131

Q

QE. See Quantitative Easing
Quantitative Easing, 6
queue jumping, 44
quote stuffing, 30, 59

R

Rajaratnam, Raj, 10
rebate arbitrage, 27
records, keeping, 110
registered market makers, 26
relative value arbitrage, 27
Renaissance Technologies, 16, 17
retail investors. See individual
    investors
revenge trading, 90, 119
ride winners, 119
Rosenblatt Securities, 64

S

S&P 500 E-Mini futures, 34, 37
SAC Capital, 11
    guilty plea, 11
Sakakibara, Eisuke, 7
scalpers, 67, 72
    futures, 55–56
    HFT, 54
    human, 57
scandals, 26
scared money syndrome, 109
Schneiderman, Eric, 47
shakeout, 112
short covering rallies, 81
shorting, 80–82
short-term traders, 67, 119
Simons, James, 16, 17
Singapore, 19
SIP, 30
slippage, 121
Soros, George, 8

sovereign wealth funds, 1, 78
special data feeds, 52
special order types, 44
    2000 industry wide, 46
    80-plus order types, 45
specialists, 26, 36
specialize, 114
speed advantage, seeking, 53
spoofing, 30, 32
spread, 25
SPY, 34
statistical arbitrage, 27
stock ticker machines, 52
stop loss levels, 120
stop orders, 41, 60, 120
    gunning, 122
    hard, 121
    If-Not-Correct, 107
    INC, 107
    mental stops, 60, 121
    predetermined, 107
    trailing, 116
strategies, 25, 31
    arbitrage, 27
    directional, 28
    manipulative, 33
    market making, 25
    momentum, 28
stub quotes, 50
super traders, 125

T

telegraph, 52
Templeton, Sir John, 97
Thatcher, Margaret, 7

Thomson Reuters, 47
To Catch a Trader, 12
trading rules
    breaking, 113
    how to follow, 125
    introduction, 85
trailing stop order, 99, 116
traps, 112
trend, follow primary, 92
Tudor Jones, Paul, 94
Turner, Lord Adair, 8
Twitter, 29

U

U.K. regulator, 12

V

Vanguard Group, 23, 49, 66
volatility, 102, 115
volatility/momentum interrupters,
    40, 56
volume, 114
volumes globally, 20

W

Wall Street Code, The, 48
winning percentage, 19
wiretaps, 10
world's reserve currency, 8

Y

Yen, 6, 8
    weakening, 6

Z

Zero Hedge, 22